EASY SEWING FOR CHILDREN
BY LEILA ALBALA

D0943277

THIRD EDITION, COMPLETELY REVISED

ALPEL PUBLISHING, CHAMBLY, QUEBEC, CANADA

EASY SEWING FOR CHILDREN
by Leila Albala
Third edition, completely revised

Published by: ALPEL PUBLISHING
P.O.Box 203, Chambly, Quebec J3L 4B3, Canada
Tel. (514) 658-6205

Other books by Leila Albala:
Easy Sewing for Infants (70 patterns)
Easy Sewing for Adults (78 patterns)
Easy Halloween Costumes for Children (60 costumes)
Costumes d'Halloween Pour Enfants (French edition)
Catalogue of Canadian Catalogues

Layout by Elie Albala

Cover design by Albert Albala

Canadian Cataloguing in Publication Data

  Albala, Leila
    Easy sewing for children

  3rd ed.
  Includes index.
  ISBN 0-921993-01-3

  1. Children's clothing. 2. Sewing.
  I. Title.

  TT635.A4 1988   646.4'06   C87-090274-1

Printed in Canada

IF YOU LIKE THIS BOOK, YOU ARE IN GOOD COMPANY

"Easy enlargement, expert sewing tips." (**Family Circle**)

"Given the price of patterns today, this is a boon to all mothers/grandmothers/aunts (and all their male counterparts) who sew. Take the basic idea and run with it." (**Canadian Book Review Annual**)

"My kind of pattern book. Beautifully organized, you can read it like a menu - and count up your savings at the same time." (**Kathy Faryon, Times Colonist**)

"Straightforward, no-nonsense presentation of material, easy-do layouts of diagrams, clear directions, easy to adapt, change or modify." (**Catalog Sources, News & Updates**)

"Excellent basic patterns, easy to follow, guarantee they'll save you money, splendid system for enlarging patterns." (**Crafts Review, The Best and Newest in Craft Supplies and Products**)

"Large selection of patterns, nicely illustrated." (**National Home Business Report**)

"Without doubt the best self-published books I have ever encountered and just as good as any of the professional sewing books on the market." (**Hands Magazine**)

"Can't imagine life without Leila's books." (**Joyce Schimmel**)

"Proved their worth many times over, common-sense approach most refreshing. More, more!!" (**D. Forrest Wilton**)

"Your book has been more useful than all my other sewing books!" (**Lise Aumais**)

"I am a total amateur at sewing but can follow your patterns so easily. I am impressed!" (**M. Marth**)

"Inspired by simplicity and common-sense approach." (**D. Attenborough**)

"Very easy, just perfect for me." (**Nicole Roy**)

"My daughter and I are having a wonderful togetherness time with the patterns." (**F.E. Boechler**)

"Your books are great, especially for children. I don't always want an elaborate pattern. I want to finish it before they grow out of it!" (**Ann Doucet**)

"Hallelujah at long last!!!" (**Cathy Stuart**)

ACKNOWLEDGEMENTS

It is easy and enjoyable to write this page, acknowledging with pleasure my family and friends, who have contributed in many ways to make this book possible.

My whole family has been understanding and patient with my hectic schedule and total preoccupation during the months that it took to put this book together. My husband and business partner, Elie, shares with me all aspects, responsibilities and work load of our publishing business. Our children, Albert and Rina, have been a daily source of inspiration as well as cheerful models for these designs.

Aside from my own children, I would also like to thank Angelica, Saila, Topi, Nathalie, Marc, Martin, and their mothers, and especially my good friends, Juliet Gauthier, Betty Racine and Shelly Fabian, for all their help. Special thanks to Jeanette Paul for her dedicated copyediting and proofreading.

Finally, thank you, my readers. Your supportive and enthusiastic letters have given me an incredible amount of energy and encouragement as well as a perfect reason to continue writing these pattern books.

With love and gratitude, I am dedicating this book to my parents. They gave me self-confidence and taught me the joy of completed work.

Leila Albala

VISUAL PATTERN INDEX

PATTERN NUMBER UNDER EACH DESIGN.   PAGE NUMBER IN PARENTHESIS.

3 YEARS up to 94 cm (37")							
1(60)	2(60)	3(60)	4(62) 4(62)	5(62)	6(62)	7(64)	
8(64)	9(64)	10(66)	10(66)	11(66)	12(68)	13(68)	14(70) 15(70)

4 YEARS up to 102 cm (40")							
16(72)	17(72)	17(72)	18(74)	19(74)	20(76)	21(76)	22(76) 23(78)
23(78)	24(78)	25(80) 25(80)	26(80)	27(82)	28(82) 20(02)	29(84)	30(84)

6 YEARS up to 119 cm (47")							
31(86)	32(86)	33(86)	34(00)	35(88)	36(88)	37(90)	38(90)
39(92)	40(92)	41(92)	42(94)	42(94)	43(94)	44(96)	45(96)

8 YEARS up to 132 cm (52")							
46(98)	47(98)	48(98)	49(98)	50(100)	51(100)	52(102)	53(102)
54(104)	54(104)	55(104)	56(106)	57(106)	58(108)	59(110)	60(110)

10 YEARS up to 142 cm (56")							
61(112)	61(112)	62(112)	63(114)	64(116)	65(116)	66(116)	67(118) 68(120)
69(120)	70(122)	71(122)	72(124)	73(124)	74(126)	75(126) 75(126)	

5

CONTENTS

PATTERNS FOR THREE-YEAR-OLDS

PATTERNS FOR FOUR-YEAR-OLDS

PATTERNS FOR SIX-YEAR-OLDS

PATTERNS FOR EIGHT-YEAR-OLDS

PATTERNS FOR TEN-YEAR-OLDS

TO THE READER

Welcome to the world of miniature patterns. Whether you are an old pro or a beginner, you will discover that it is a smart, "new" way of pattern-making. While I cannot claim to have invented miniature patterns, it is unusual to find a whole book full of them. Although they have been popular in Scandinavia and many European countries for years, I was cautioned that Canadian and American sewers insist on full-size patterns. I decided, however, to take the risk with a pattern book for infants firmly believing there must be a few sewers interested in the miniature method. And there are. Not just a few, but more than 40,000 ordered my book after reading about it in Family Circle, Vogue Patterns, and several other magazines. That first pattern book has grown into a series of books. They are still available by mail order, and now through many public libraries, book stores and fabric outlets, too.

I am particularly pleased by the testimonials from some of my readers who had no previous experience with miniature patterns (or sewing either!), and yet had enough courage and curiosity to try them. They were rewarded by the discovery that this is an easy and creative method. Each miniature pattern takes only minutes to enlarge.

A huge, ever-growing pile of letters from my readers never fails to give me energy and encouragement. This positive demand for miniature patterns reflects my own desire to have such books myself. It is practical to have a large selection of basic, versatile patterns on hand. This book saves time and money, not only in isolated areas, but for busy and creative hands everywhere.

I wish each one of you, my sewing friends, happy and ever easier sewing!

BEFORE YOU START

Before using the patterns in this book, read the text pages with a highlighter pen in hand. Mark all the information that's new and important to you.

For your convenience, I have arranged each pattern and its sewing instructions on adjoining pages. As a bonus, I filled any leftover space with useful sewing tips.

Use the handy index at the end of this book to find any specific information you need.

ENLARGING MINIATURE PATTERNS

To include a large selection of designs in my books, each pattern is reduced in size and printed on a miniature grid.

"Easy Sewing for Infants": One square = 2.5cm (1")
"Easy Sewing for Children": One square = 2.5cm (1")
"Easy Sewing for Adults": One square = 5cm (2")

Enlarge miniature patterns to full-size grid by marking all corners, and then connecting them dot-to-dot with lines as shown in the miniature pattern. Once you get used to it, each pattern takes just minutes to enlarge.

The easiest way to enlarge miniature patterns is by taping a sheet of tracing paper on a cardboard cutting board that is marked with a grid. Since the lines on a cardboard cutting board are marked 2½cm (1") apart, reinforce every second line with a black marker so you will also have a 5cm (2") grid for adult patterns.

Or make yourself a handy "master grid" from a large sheet of paper or white vinyl. Draw a grid of squares (2½cm/1") by using a long ruler and a black marker. (Use waterproof marker for vinyl.) If you draw every second line dotted (or use different color), you also have a 5cm (2") grid for adult patterns. Tape a sheet of tracing paper onto your "master grid" (the grid is visible through the paper) and enlarge the miniature patterns (as well as make any alterations) directly onto the tracing paper. The grid remains clean and reusable for years to come. Roll it up for easy storage into any cardboard tube. As a bonus, your "master grid" can be used to enlarge miniature patterns for toys and crafts published in many magazines. Ready-made vinyl grids are also available commercially.

Some fabric stores sell pattern paper or non-woven material (looks like interfacing) marked with dots that are spaced 2.5cm (1") apart. Such paper or material can be used to enlarge miniature patterns by connecting the dots for a grid.

When enlarging many patterns, it is practical to have a good supply of tracing paper on hand. Your local art supply retailer sells tracing paper in large rolls.

Alternatives to tracing paper:

Crinkle-type plastic bags (semi-transparent) that the stores use for your fabrics and other purchases make handy "tracing paper" at literally no cost. Open the bags out flat and tape them together side-by-side. Get your family and friends to collect a supply of such bags for you.

Tissue paper (sheets used for gift wrapping) or wax paper can be used as tracing paper. Tape sheets together.

Old commercial patterns. Here's a source of perfect tracing paper that just might be sitting idle in your house, if you are absolutely sure never to need those patterns again. You might also find commercial patterns for pennies at garage and rummage sales, thrift shops, and your local sewing supply store. The tissue paper sheets are conveniently large so, by ignoring all lines and markings on them and by using bright felt markers, you can use the sheets for your own patterns.

Sometimes you can save pattern paper by enlarging only a part of a pattern. For this reason, I have drawn only half of the patterns (even sleeves) that have identical other halves. When back and front are identical except for neckline (and sometimes front edges too), I have drawn them as one so you need to enlarge only one pattern piece instead of two. (See "Cutting the fabric" for more information.) When the pattern is long and straight or even slightly flared from underarms to hem (such as a dress, long nightgown, T-shirt, bathrobe), enlarge the pattern for the upper part only, and extend cutting lines for the rest directly onto the fabric.

When the pattern is very easy, square or rectangle, such as a gathered skirt, ruffle, waistband or pocket, enlarge it directly onto the fabric to save time and pattern paper. If you are inexperienced in this and afraid that you wouldn't have enough fabric if you cut it without a proper plan, first make a miniature cutting layout with proportional dimensions on any squared paper.

SAVE THE PATTERNS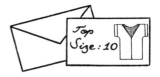

You will hopefully be able to use many of these patterns several times because, with different fabrics, trims, and variations mentioned in patterns, you can create several different garments from every pattern. The pattern sizes are easy to enlarge and reduce when necessary. Fold the enlarged patterns neatly into separate envelopes (used envelopes are fine), and mention the pattern name, number, size, and the page number of this book for easy reference on each envelope. Mention pattern numbers also on each pattern piece in case they get mixed up. Straighten out folded pattern pieces with warm iron.

FABRIC REQUIREMENTS
SUGGESTED FABRICS

There are no cutting layouts in this book because they would take up so much space that I would have to eliminate many patterns. I have mentioned the fabric requirements for the most likely, or most convenient fabric width for each pattern, always mentioning first the length and then the width. If you use fabric of different width, calculate from the miniature or the enlarged pattern, how much fabric is needed, or take this book or the enlarged pattern with you to the store. Better yet, adopt my style of sewing and stock up on fabrics at home in larger quantities, and then let the fabrics inspire you to see what can be made out of them. Then cut out several garments one day, and sew them the next.

Suggested fabrics are listed for every garment, but be inventive and adventurous and use fabrics of your choice. If you wish to use non-stretch fabric for a pattern designed for stretch fabrics only, enlarge the pattern slightly to add sufficient ease. When using stretch fabrics for a pattern designed for non-stretch fabrics, eliminate seam allowances or reduce the pattern slightly in width if you find it necessary (depending on design).

Extra fabric may be required for stripes, plaids, or one-way designs or for fabric with one-way nap. Fabric requirements are listed only for original design, not for variations mentioned in the brackets. Notions needed to complete each garment (except the thread) are listed.

SIMPLE INSTRUCTIONS

Instructions for completing each garment are purposely kept short and simple to encourage you to realize how easy, uncomplicated, and pleasant sewing can be. Naturally you need to know basic sewing techniques before using patterns with such brief instructions. Let the work guide you rather than intimidate you, and use common sense to solve the little problems that may surface. Practice, of course, is your very best teacher and, although I have been sewing all my life, I am humbly learning all the time.

If you are an inexperienced seamstress, ask a sewing friend for help to give you the confidence so necessary in the beginning. Buy yourself at least one really good sewing instruction book with a comprehensive index, so you'll have your own private teacher at all times. I have several good books with detailed, professional illustrations and up-to-date, easy to understand know-how about practically everything concerning sewing. They are my endless source of useful information.

In order to include so many patterns in this book, I have saved space by using brief, non-repetitive directions. After getting used to this style of sewing, I am confident you will be able to sew without any directions.

It is important to read the text part of this book because I keep referring to it frequently.

Rib knits: See "Rib knit bands".

Patch pockets: Overlock upper edge, fold it under 2.5cm (1") with right sides together, stitch folded ends closed, turn right side out, press, and topstitch upper edge down. Press seam allowances under on both sides and lower edge. Topstitch pockets in place. When sewing a pocket with curved corners, stitch upper edge as explained above, then baste around curves and pull the thread so that the curves turn neatly under; press seam allowances under and topstitch the pocket in place.

Ruffles: When sewing a ruffle to skirt lower edge, stitch ruffle pieces together into a circle. Narrowly hem the lower edge of ruffle, or trim it with lace. Sew two rows of long gathering stitches, close to each other, to ruffle upper edge. Divide both ruffle upper edge and skirt lower edge into equal parts (four to eight sections, depending on skirt width) and mark the sections with pins. With right sides together, match markings, and pin ruffle to garment. Pull bobbin threads of gathering stitches to gather ruffle edge, so that it will match the garment's edge, distributing the fullness evenly. Stitch ruffle to the garment, with gathers up against the presser foot. Zigzag or overlock raw edges of seam allowances together.

Overlock: To cleanfinish raw edges of pocket tops, lower edge of garment, sleeve ends, and facings, overlock (or zigzag) the edge prior to topstitching it in place. This fast and neat method also helps you to avoid excessive bulk since you don't need to fold the raw edges under.

METRIC AND IMPERIAL MEASUREMENTS

This book provides you with both metric and imperial measurements. I always mention first the metric, then the equivalent imperial measurement.

The measurements may differ slightly and, for practical purposes, show rounded figures, but the difference is irrelevant. Confidently choose either system and ignore the other one.

For your convenience, I have listed below fractions of an inch frequently used in sewing and their metric equivalents.

Metric	Imperial
3 mm	1/8"
5 mm	3/16"
6 mm	1/4"
1 cm	3/8"
1.3 cm	1/2"
1.5 cm	5/8"
2 cm	3/4"
2.5 cm	1"

SEWING MACHINES

When I once stayed in Switzerland for two years, I was like an orphan without my sewing machine. Fortunately I found a very old sewing machine at a flea market (for five dollars!). It was one of those non-electric, unbreakable, basic models with a large, decorative table and straight stitch only. I managed to get the tension so good that I was able to sew my wedding gown, winter coat, and many other lovely garments.

With a few other machines since then, I have learned a lot along the way. Choosing the best machine for your purposes is both time consuming and very difficult when the choice is so large. When the time came to buy "the best sewing machine in the world", I decided to take the task seriously in order not to regret my decision. I read the whole Consumer Guide book on sewing machines, tested a dozen different machines, attended demonstrations, had home trials, and questioned everybody I knew who sews. It took several months of active, dedicated searching to find a machine that has been sewing with me without a complaint for well over ten years. Of course there are many other good machines on the market apart from my choice, so it is indeed well worth your time to decide carefully which one of them will be your sewing partner perhaps for the rest of your life.

To compare different models, test as many machines as possible. Be firm and don't let an aggressive salesperson talk you into buying a machine before you have seen several, and have had time to think over your decision. Just the fact that a sewing machine is sold at a discount for a limited time shouldn't push you into buying it unless you would choose that one anyway.

If possible, have a demonstration at home so you can take extra time trying it out in peace. Sometimes you may be allowed to keep the machine at home for a trial period free of obligation. If you do this, be sure you will not be intimidated into buying that machine if you are not absolutely sure you want it. Another good reason to test the machine at home is to check how noisy it is in the home environment. There are often so many people and so much noise in stores that it is impossible to properly hear how much noise the machine makes.

Even more important than noise is, of course, the stitch. To check the tension properly, you should have your own fabric samples including heavy-weight fabrics, lightweight knits, and difficult-to-sew sheers. Stores will give you samples but, because they are usually firm cotton, they will show a good stitch with any machine. To be sure the tension is correct, the stitch should lock between the two layers of fabric, and the link should not be visible on either side. A balanced tension shows even stitches on both sides of fabric. For testing, use fabric samples of solid colors and threads in contrasting colors to make the stitch and any faults more visible. Experiment and adjust the upper thread tension without fear, as well as the bobbin thread tension, until you get desired results. Surprisingly enough, many sewing machine salespeople don't know enough about thread tension, sewing stretchy fabrics, or uses of different needles. To adjust the bobbin thread tension, gradually turn the thread tension knob in the bobbin case until you get a good tension. Take along a sewing friend who knows how to test a machine if you are inexperienced yourself.

Freearm is so useful and necessary that I wouldn't recommend buying a machine without it. Even if you have to pay extra, you won't regret it.

A second-hand machine is a good way to start but only if you manage to get good tension with it. Buying a bad sewing machine could be quite discouraging and could make one "allergic to sewing".

In recent years, many inexpensive and yet surprisingly good machines with convenient utility stitches (including various overlock and stretch stitches) have come onto the market. It is not that important to have several decorative, fancy stitches in a sewing machine (because how many times, really, would you want to sew little dogs or whatever running in a row?). If you are shopping for an inexpensive sewing machine, choose one with good straight stitch, with forward and backward movements, zigzag, stretch stitch, built-in buttonholer, blind stitch, and freearm. They are the most essential features, all else is extra. Also try to get at least one "quick seam" or overlock. It's a stitch that sews the seam and finishes the raw edges simultaneously so you don't have to go down the seam twice. You will be using it a lot. (See the chapter "Stretchy Sewing" for improvised quick seam.)

I often think that if husbands realized how much home-sewing saves, they would run to buy the best machine. Some smart men even sew themselves. Impress your husband by showing him the beautiful garments you can create and sew something for him too. He will have every reason to encourage you and to regard you as a talented lady with golden hands.

Are you already wild about sergers? After I found out about sergers (also called overlock machines),

I went to see one. When I had searched several months for just the right sewing machine, I bought my serger after just five minutes of demonstration. I was so impressed and I still am. The machine itself is small and doesn't look at all impressive. In fact, you wouldn't even believe it is a sewing machine. However, it is a small miracle, saves lots of time, and makes sewing fun. There are several different sergers now on the market and, even if you don't intend to buy one, it is most interesting just to see how they work. Yet a word of caution is necessary here. Don't rush to buy one as your only sewing machine because it just sews seams. Therefore, first you need to buy a regular sewing machine.

My serger has two needles, a knife, and four huge spools of thread. The thread can be a problem because it is expensive to buy large cones of thread in several colors and four of each. But, if you have basic colors, they will blend into almost any fabric and will last for a long time. In a pinch, use blending colored threads just for the chainstitch and whatever you have on hand for the overlock. Factories and factory outlets sometimes sell half-empty cones for pennies. Sergers have no bobbin which, you can imagine, is just wonderful for uninterrupted sewing. One needle sews straight chainstitch, while the other one overlocks the edges that are trimmed simultaneously by the knife. The result is a very neat and professional narrow seam. The machine is so amazingly fast that it is now possible to whip up several garments in a few hours.

When buying a sewing machine or serger, inquire about availability of parts and service, guarantee, and free instructions. Take a course in its use, if available, even if you think you know enough about sewing. I was surprised at how much I learned.

Care for your machine and it will reward you with enjoyable and troublefree sewing. Lubricate it regularly and be sure to use only good quality machine oil. I mention this because I heard about one lady who used cooking oil (would you believe!) for her brand new machine. The result was such a mess that even the guarantee did not pay for the repair. When my machine is tired, noisy, and slow, I give it a good cleaning and oiling, change the needle, and it works like a charm again.

Protect your machine from dust by covering it when not in use. If you don't have a special turndown table, or don't always put the machine away in its carrying case, make a pretty little quilt or coverlet and remember to use it. When you leave the machine, turn it off (or unplug it), especially if you have children in the house.

Clogging and jamming are caused by fabric or thread ends being drawn down into the bobbin compartment. It is most annoying. You can virtually eliminate it by practicing these tips. Change the machine needle frequently. When placing the fabric under the presser foot, turn the handwheel so that the take-up lever is in its highest position and the needle is on its way down with the first stitch. Hold the thread ends firmly and taut to the back. Turn the wheel by hand until the needle goes into the fabric. When sewing sheer or difficult fabrics or lightweight knits, backstitching at the beginning and end of the seam may pull the fabric into the needleplate hole. So, slip a piece of typing paper between the fabric and needleplate to get a good start; rip the paper off after sewing.

If jamming occurs in spite of these tricks, take your time to carefully remove the fabric so it won't tear. If gentle pulling doesn't release the fabric from the needleplate hole, unscrew the needle or remove the bobbin case (if not blocked by the needle) or try removing the needleplate.

Be sure to frequently brush away the packed lint that constantly accumulates around the bobbin compartment and under the needleplate. It can clog the machine and cause stitching problems such as jamming, thread breakage, poorly formed stitches, and it can interfere with dropfeed control. If the needle keeps running despite the fact that you have loosened the handwheel for winding the thread on bobbin, undo the handwheel screw, remove outer part and drop a bit of oil into the handwheel bearing. When you stop sewing even for a few seconds, and even in the middle of a seam, learn to take your foot completely off the pedal. Even the lightest touch on the pedal will tease the motor, eventually causing damage which is expensive to repair.

Read your sewing machine manual carefully and refer to it frequently. Particularly useful is the section which explains possible reasons for common sewing machine problems. A few good tricks can save you many expensive and inconvenient trips to a repair shop.

You will be using the sewing machine more often if it is easily available. If possible, have a place where you can leave the machine as is, in case you have to interrupt your work. When my second child was born, she took over my sewing room. Consequently, I found it too inconvenient to store the machine in a closet or to set it on the kitchen table, only to clear it away again for mealtimes. I found myself using it less and less, until I found a solution. While awaiting the sewing room of my dreams in the basement, I sewed in the bedroom. There I had a handy desk, a comfortable chair, and good lighting to encourage me to use the machine again practically daily.

FABRICS

We are lucky with such a beautiful and abundant, often even bewildering choice of fabrics on the market. It's nice to go shopping for just the right fabric in a well-equipped store, but to save time and money I usually stock up fabrics at home, not only for children's clothes, but for the whole family. I enjoy shopping at factory outlets and discount halls and, when I find fabrics I like at a bargain price, I buy lots of them in different colors (a few metres or yards each), even if I don't know right at that moment what I will make out of them. By using fabrics in two or three solid colors or prints that go well together, I make several different garments out of each and then can mix and match them endlessly.

If there is a garment factory near you, check if they sell any leftover fabrics, threads and other notions, and you might well have found your own treasure chest to return to again and again. Bankruptcy sales (or closing of business) should be your favorites too, if you like bargains. If you live in an isolated area, you probably will find it well worth the trip to drive even a longer distance for a carload of rock-bottom priced fabrics. Take your sewing friends along to share the fun and expenses.

Even my husband has recently become quite an expert on fabrics and often surprises me with beautiful fabrics he finds at sales and factories. Aside from praising him for what a wonderful guy he is, I always let him know which fabrics I like the best to ensure that the future surprises are even more successful.

I also check remnant counters for discontinued fabrics, ends of rolls, and pieces with a small flaw. Remnants are often just the right size for kids' clothes and, by combining two or more colors, I can create unique garments for pennies. I always keep a measuring tape in my shopping bag, as well as current measurements of my children. Clever cutting saves a lot of fabric, so it is best to learn to figure out how much is needed. It is easy with a little practice.

It takes imagination to discover the real treasures among the rest of the cheap fabrics which may often look like a pile of junk, but it can be interesting and certainly well worth all the trouble. Sometimes bargain fabrics need to be washed and ironed before you can fully appreciate them and recognize their true potential. In fact, prior to cutting it is wise to wash (or thoroughly soak) all fabrics to preshrink them, unless you are absolutely sure they will not shrink.

Prewashing serves other purposes too. Some fabrics are pressed off-grain and might be sold at a low price just for that reason. To straighten them, you may need to dampen such fabrics. Stretch gently on the bias and press, if necessary. Often washing sets the fibers straight without trouble. That's why a garment sewn from off-grain fabric appears twisted after washing. If you can't wash or iron out the pressed foldline, avoid that when cutting out the fabric. Or place crease where it is not too visible, or underneath ribbon trim (down center of sweatshirt sleeves or sides of pull-on pants). Fabrics printed off-grain are impossible to straighten. Prewashing also removes finishes that may cause skipped stitches.

It may seem such a pity to wash or even just soak new fabrics especially since they are probably clean. However, I have never regretted doing so, whereas I have made my share of mistakes by sewing garments without preshrinking the fabric, only to have an unpleasant surprise after the first wash. Fabrics most likely to shrink are made of 100% cotton. If you buy a very long piece of fabric (more than three metres or yards), don't wash it in one piece because it will get twisted and tangled into a discouraging mess in washer and dryer. Instead, cut a piece long enough for a garment, measure it carefully in both length and width, and wash and dry it. If it doesn't shrink, you don't need to wash the rest (unless dirty or pressed off-grain). If it shrinks, cut the rest into pieces of two to three metres or yards each, and preshrink them too. Another smart way to preshrink a long piece of fabric is to fold it neatly (accordion style) into a bathtub full of water, soak it thoroughly and let it drip-dry over a wooden rod extended over the tub. Iron if necessary prior to cutting it out to recapture that store-bought crispness.

If you buy stretch fabric knitted into a tube without selvages (or with selvages sewn together), preshrink it that way to prevent the edges from curling. If you preshrink fabrics that ravel easily, zigzag or overlock all cut edges first.

Sometimes you can make beautiful clothes for children out of grownups' old clothes for literally no cost. Your old T-shirts can have a beautiful comeback turned into tiny garments. Men's old undershirts, soft and lintfree from repeated washings, would be just perfect for infants' underwear. Don't bother undoing old seams, just cut them off. Check both right and wrong side of fabric and use the better one. Many of my readers write that they buy second-hand clothes for pennies from garage sales to transform into new garments. That is a wonderful way of recycling our resources. Also rescue all good buttons, belt buckles and zippers from discarded garments. It is even fashionable to go back to basics, to stop wasting, and to do anything with your hands, so you can proudly brag about your creative ideas and savings to your envious friends! Better yet, get together to share ideas, to sew, and to have a good time.

I have dozens of bargain fabrics at home. When the inspiration hits me, I cut out several garments one day and sew them the next. It's just like preparing many dishes at the same time for the freezer. When you buy fabrics that you don't use right away, don't hide them in bags in lost places to be forgotten. Fold them neatly on a closet shelf or in a drawer where they are easily accessible and visible to inspire you. Stop feeling guilty about all those bargain fabrics accumulating in your sewing corner! Don't feel you must sew them into something right away. "Fabric addiction" is quite enjoyable and harmless and you are entitled to a few "collection errors" on your way to creative sewing.

My favorite fabrics are 100% cottons (including corduroy, Indian cotton, seersucker, eyelet, batiste, etc.), cotton knits (unfortunately hard to find so I often have to settle for cotton-polyester blends), stretch terry, velour, fleece (woven or sweatshirt fabrics), and quilted fabrics. They are easy-care, wash-and-wear type fabrics, easy to sew, comfortable to wear, and they look nice. For adult clothes, I also use silk types, crepe de chine, wool flannel, jersey, and fine wool or blends. Flame-retardant fabrics are required by law on children's sleepwear.

THREAD

Thread is as important as the fabric. It's false economy to use poor quality thread. It may break when sewing and washing because it is not strong enough. It may have knots and snags or it may not be colorfast. Use good quality thread and, if you have not yet tried cotton wrapped polyester thread, you are in for a pleasant surprise. It has combined the good qualities of both cotton and polyester and sews smoothly with tanglefree, slightly stretchy results.

I keep a supply of basic colors on hand so I don't have to rush to the store just for thread every time I feel like sewing.

For best results and correct tension, use the same thread both in the needle and bobbin. Polyester thread frays easily when broken. It should, therefore, be cut with scissors on a slant so it will be easier to thread the needle.

Does your upper thread often get wound up around the spool-holder underneath the spool? So annoying! Prevent it by sewing a simple tube from cotton knit or rib knit. Make the tube as high as the spool and loose enough so that the spool can turn easily inside it. With slit rim of spool at bottom (so thread doesn't get caught in the slit), slip the tube around the spool with thread running from the top. This tube will save you much frustration and is reusable for all the spools of same size. While you are at it, make a few extras as gifts for friends.

MACHINE NEEDLES

Change blunt or bent machine needles immediately and, for all stretch fabrics, use ballpoint needles or universal point needles. The universal point needle is practical for "lazy sewers" since it can be used on both knits and wovens. Regular needles break stretchy fibers and cause holes and runs. Change the needle to a smaller size when sewing lightweight fabrics.

Machine needles should be replaced frequently when sewing synthetic fabrics because synthetic fibers are more abrasive than natural fibers and dull the needle rapidly. Dull needles may cause bad or skipped stitches, puckered seams, thread breakage, tangling of thread and small tears in fiber, causing runs. Although the cause may be elsewhere, try changing the needle first if you have any of those problems.

PINS

Have a good supply of rustfree, sharp pins. I love extra-long pins with large colored balls. They are designed for knits and thick fabrics, but I use them for practically everything. Basting is time consuming so save it for complicated designs that must be fitted. For the easy designs in this book, with a little practice, pins work just as well. Pin the seams conveniently crosswise with the pin heads to the right, so you can pull the pins out without stopping the machine just before the presser foot starts sliding over the pin. If you use smaller pins and fairly long stitches and have a "hinged" presser foot, you can also stitch right across pins, but I would not recommend it since it may dull the machine needle quickly. For short seams, it is easy to sew not only without basting but without pins as well.

SCISSORS

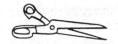

Buy the best quality steel scissors and you'll enjoy them for years to come. Remember, you are saving so much money by sewing that you deserve the best tools you can buy. Spread the word that good sewing tools make excellent gifts.

You will need a large pair for cutting out fabrics, and small ones for snipping thread ends and trimming seams. Have your scissors sharpened regularly. For smooth cutting without creaking, squeeze a drop of machine oil into the screw where the blades cross as soon as you buy the scissors, and once or twice a year thereafter.

To keep your sewing scissors sharp for a long time, use them only for fabrics. Have another pair for cutting out paper.

BUTTONS, ZIPPERS, ETC.

If you have to drive to a store just to buy a set of buttons, they may end up costing more than the fabric, besides taking too much time. I bought a two-pound bag of hundreds of assorted buttons years ago for a dollar, and have been using them for countless garments, especially for children's clothes. As a bonus, my son played with them for years, sorting the buttons out by color and size, counting them and "goldmining" the prettiest ones. I almost did not buy that bag for those unusual, crazy and glimmering buttons, because I thought I could not possibly use them for anything. For a child with a healthy dose of imagination, they are gold nuggets and diamonds. Now that my little daughter is old enough not to put the buttons in her mouth, my collection is inspiring her, too, in many happy games while I am sewing. Not bad for an inexpensive bag of buttons! I now keep refilling my button box from time to time.

Whenever there is a sale particularly a clearance sale, I buy zippers, bias tape, ribbons, wide elastic, appliqués, or whatever I happen to find at a real bargain-price for future use. Sometimes a large, beautiful zipper with an interesting, decorative tab inspires me to create a whole garment around it.

Regard sewing the same way as you do cooking. You need staples at home to be creative any time you get an inspiration.

CUTTING THE FABRIC

Fold the fabric lengthwise in half, right sides together, or fold twice so that the selvages meet at center or off-center (depending on pattern pieces to be cut). Read instructions for every pattern carefully, and place the pattern pieces as directed. For stretch fabrics, the straight arrow must be placed on the straight lengthwise grain of the fabric so that the width will be stretchy. You also could cut striped fabric on the bias. Spandex is stretchy both ways, but if the maximum stretch is in the length (unlike other stretch fabrics), cut maillots, bodysuits, and swimtrunks so that the fabric length goes around the body.

It is very important to cut the fabric out on the straight grain, because otherwise the garment will appear twisted. As mentioned earlier, dampen the fabric to straighten the grainline, pull on the bias and press, if necessary.

Many stretch fabrics tend to curl around cut edges. It is annoying to stitch such edges together. You can partly eliminate this problem by handling the cut edges as little as possible, and avoid pulling and stretching them after cutting. Use lots of pins (or good old basting) to straighten the curly edges prior to sewing.

Pin the pattern pieces on folded fabric. Mark the cutting lines with tailor's chalk. With a little practice, you can skip marking the cutting line and simply cut directly along the pattern edge. Instead of pins, you can use some weights (such as books or canned foods) to hold the pattern pieces in place.

When cutting out fabrics with one-way nap (such as velour, terry, corduroy, velvet, velveteen), be sure to have the nap running downward for every pattern piece, for a smooth touch and even color. Otherwise it will look as if you have cut the pattern pieces from two different shades. I have seen many commercial patterns and sewing books instruct you to cut the nap upward for deeper shade. However, I have always regretted cutting the fabric that way because it felt rough and unpleasant to touch.

Test if knit fabric runs and if so, in which direction. It is wise to cut the pattern so that it will run upwards from where there is less pressure on garment (such as hemline instead of shoulders, or sleeve ends instead of sleeve tops).

Follow grainline indications on the pattern pieces carefully, especially when cutting stretch fabrics. Remember that the stretchy crosswise grain must almost always go around the body (or perhaps cut on the bias for striped knits), not up and down. Occasionally the fabric is sufficiently stretchy in both length and width, and then it is possible to cut the pattern either way, providing that the fabric hangs properly both ways.

Place pattern pieces that are so directed on fold and cut only the cutting lines. When you need to cut two identical but asymmetric pieces (front-halfs, raglan sleeves, kangaroo pockets), cut the pattern out of double-layered fabric, so the pieces will automatically be mirror images of each other. When you need only one piece and not on the fold, open up the fabric prior to cutting. Sometimes you save fabric by not folding it exactly in half, so it is wise to plan the layout carefully for all pieces prior to cutting.

To save time and pattern paper, I have drawn only half of most patterns, even sleeves, that have identical other halves. However, if you want a complete sleeve pattern, enlarge the half-sleeve as shown onto folded pattern paper. When back and front are identical except for neckline, I have drawn them as one so you need to enlarge only one pattern piece instead of two. First cut two back pieces on fabric fold, remove one of them as the final back piece, and cut lower neckline for front as shown. Some patterns have identical front and back except for neckline and center front, such as jacket or coat. Enlarge the pattern with all lines as shown, cut out one back piece on fold, and then use the same pattern to cut out the two front sections along selvages of the fabric.

SEWING STRETCHY

Stretch fabrics are easy to sew, they fit well, don't show wrinkles, and they give neat results with a little experience and know-how. You don't need to leave much ease for action and comfort since the stretchy ease is built right into the fabric itself.

Whenever you sew stretch fabrics, use a ballpoint or universal point needle, polyester or cotton-wrapped polyester thread, and stretch stitch (or overlock, quick seam, or tiny zigzag). If your machine only has a straight stitch, you must stretch the fabric as you sew and stitch the seams twice.

Improvised quick seam: One version of "quick seam" can be sewn with the same stitch that you would use for blind hem stitch. So, even if your sewing machine manual doesn't tell you that, you can use the blind hem stitch as a quick seam for lightweight stretch fabrics. Keep the raw edges to the left (unlike most other sewing), adjust the stitch width to the widest, and the stitch length as short as desired.

Use shortcuts whenever possible in cutting and sewing, but it is worth it to take extra time to topstitch neatly and to match stripes and plaids for perfect results. I like topstitching with a double needle for facings around neck openings, sleeve ends, hems, and pockets. A double needle gives professional and neat results so easily.

ELASTICS

Elastics are practical and easy to apply when you know a few tips for neat and comfortable results. Elastic should never be too tight because restricting blood circulation is both harmful and painful.

Self-casing: Use this method when you don't use topstitched elastic (described later) for shorts, pull-on pants, pull-on skirt waist, sleeve and leg ends. Overlock the raw edge of fabric and press it to inside, stitch close to raw edge forming a casing and leaving an opening for elastic. Cut elastic the desired length and insert it through the casing with safety pin or bodkin. Make sure the elastic is not twisted (it's helpful to mark both ends of "right side" prior to inserting the elastic through the casing). Join the ends without overlapping and stitch them together securely by machine or hand. Don't use a knot to tie the ends together. Stitch opening closed. To prevent elastic from rolling, stitch elastic along seams (stitch-in-ditch) through all thicknesses. These stitches will not be visible. (Sew casing around neck opening with facing or extra-wide bias tape.)

Elasticized waistline with or without casing: When elasticizing the waistline, use one of the following methods:

A) If there is a seam (such as joining bodice to skirt or romper top to shorts), stitch stretched elastic directly to seam allowance on the wrong side of garment.

B) If there is no seam at waist, try the garment on, and tie elastic around waist. Pull the fabric above the elastic until desired fullness is achieved. Clearly mark this line as the waistline by running a basting thread along the lower side of elastic, so you will be able to see it on the wrong side. (Do this prior to hemming the lower edge, because elasticizing the waistline will shorten the garment.) Turn the garment inside out. Zigzag stretched elastic along marked line, dividing the fullness evenly between equal sections of elastic and fabric.

C) Elastic through casing. Mark the waistline as above. Stitch a fabric strip or bias tape to the wrong side of garment along marked waistline, stitching both upper and lower edges to form a casing and leaving an opening. Insert elastic through opening and stitch elastic ends together. Stitch opening closed. Divide fullness evenly at front and back. Stitch elastic along side seams through all thicknesses to prevent it from rolling.

Topstitched elastic: This is a neat, fast and twistproof way to elasticize cut edges of waist, leg and sleeve ends, and neck opening of any garment, even swimwear. Cut elastic the desired length and, without overlapping, zigzag ends together into a circle. Divide both elastic and fabric edge into equal sections by using pins or by marking with tailor's chalk. Fabric edge even with elastic edge, zigzag elastic to the wrong side of garment. Stretch each section of elastic as needed while you sew so the garment edge lies flat. For a narrow elastic, stitch top edge only. For a wider elastic, stitch both edges. As you stitch, hold elastic taut both in front of and behind the presser foot. Turn the elasticized edge to the inside, and edgestitch from wrong side, stretching the elastic as you sew so that fabric lies flat. If desired, stitch additional rows through elastic from right side, stretching while you sew.

Depending on the width and quality of elastic and fabric used, and especially if additional topstitched rows are added, elastic ribbon will stretch when stitched through as described above. Since this type of elasticized edge is very bothersome to undo, test first on a scrap fabric with a short piece of elastic to see the results (and to get used to this method) and adjust the elastic length for the garment accordingly.

Elastic shirring by machine: If your machine has a special presser foot with a hole in it (for shirring by covering elastic thread with zigzag), follow instructions in your sewing machine manual.

Or use the following easy method. Hand-wind elastic thread around bobbin, stretching slightly. Use polyester or cotton-wrapped polyester thread (not 100% cotton) as upper thread. Stitch from the right side of garment, so the elastic bobbin thread is on the wrong side. Use long machine stitches. Test first on scrap. To mark the first row foot, fold the fabric, press forming a crease, open it up and stitch along the crease. (Or stitch first row so that the side of presser foot runs along fabric edge which has been cut on selvage or narrowly hemmed or trimmed with lace.) When stitching additional rows, hold the fabric taut both in front of and behind the presser foot. Make each row of elastic stitching so that the previous row runs along the side of presser foot. Be sure to lock each stitching line securely at the beginning and end with backward stitches (or knot thread ends securely together).

Before sewing with elastic thread, check it first to see if it is of good quality. Stretch the thread to its maximum length. If it breaks easily, return the thread to the store for an exchange. Although bad quality is quite unusual, I mention it because I once wasted hours trying to figure out what I was doing wrong.

Shirring with elastic thread in the bobbin may loosen the bobbin thread tension. If that happens, you'll have to tighten the tension afterward before sewing with regular thread again. Simply tighten the screw in the bobbin case until you get proper tension, or follow directions in your sewing machine manual.

Depending on fabric and stitch length, elastic shirring will shorten the original length of fabric (i.e. the direction in which you are sewing, whether it is along shoulder straps or around body) to about half. Therefore, if you wish to add elastic shirring to pattern pieces that are not designed for that, shirring is best done prior to cutting out the fabric.

BIAS TAPES
AND STRETCH TAPES

Bias tapes and stretch tapes are useful for binding raw edges neatly and quickly.

Bias tape is a strip of non-stretch fabric cut on the bias.

Stretch tape is a strip of stretch fabric cut across the width. It is not necessary to cut stretch fabric on the bias. Cutting across the stretchy width is more convenient and usually saves fabric too. (Exception: When binding raw edges of a stretch garment that don't have to stretch, you might find it more practical and neater to cut the strips lengthwise along non-stretchy grain.)

Ready-made, prefolded bias tape is inexpensive and available in practically any color. However, since it is made from non-stretch fabric, I find it too stiff for soft, lightweight, or stretch garments. It is easy to make your own tape from the same fabric as the garment. Or use a different fabric (such as rib knit strips) or contrasting color for a beautiful decorative effect.

Commercial bias tape is known as singlefold or doublefold. In this book I use mainly self-made tapes folded differently from store-bought ones so I use the following terms (all explained below): unifold, bifold, trifold. (Trifold tape is commercially known as doublefold.)

Making bias tapes

Cut strips of non-stretch fabric on the bias. Depending on use, press the strips unifold, bifold or trifold as explained below for stretch tapes.

Making unifold stretch tape

Cut a strip 2cm (3/4") wide (or twice the desired finished width) across the width of stretch fabric. Wrong sides in, press the strip in half lengthwise. Bind raw fabric edge with the prepared tape. Topstitch the tape in place with short but wide zigzag which will cover raw tape edges for neat and unbulky results. Unifold stretch tape is soft and pliable so it's suitable especially for children's clothes and just perfect for cotton knits, stretch terry and velour.

Making bifold stretch tape

This is a practical way to avoid bulk when sewing velour or terry (or when using bulky fabrics to make bias tapes such as corduroy). Under the fabric it will look like unifold tape, and on the top like trifold tape. Cut a strip 4½cm (1 3/4") wide (or three times the desired finished width) across the width of stretch fabric. Press one-third of width under, then press the entire strip in half lengthwise wrong sides in, so that raw edge and folded edge meet. Cleanfinish the outer raw edge with overlock. Bind raw fabric edge with the prepared tape so that the tape's folded edge is on the right side of garment. Topstitch through all thicknesses.

Making trifold stretch tape (Commercially known as doublefold)

Cut a strip 5cm (2") wide (or four times the desired

finished width) across the width of stretch fabric. Wrong sides in, press the strip in half lengthwise (to mark the center line), open it up and press both long edges to center of strip, then press the entire strip refolded on center line again. Bind raw fabric edge with the prepared tape. Topstitch it in place through all thicknesses with straight stitch, zigzag or decorative stitch. Or stitch it in place in two steps: First stitch the underseam by holding the opened-up tape under the garment, raw edges together and right side of tape against wrong side of fabric, stitching on the first fold. Now turn the tape over the edge to the right side, so that tape's center fold is binding the raw fabric edge, and the unstitched folded side of tape covers the first stitching line. Topstitch through all thicknesses. Use any stitch but, if around pullover's small neckhole, use only stretch stitch for sufficient ease and stretch.

RIB KNIT BANDS

Rib knit fabric is available by the metre (or yard) in a variety of widths and weights, and in different colors. Cut it into close-fitting bands for neck opening, waist, wrists, and ankles of T-shirts, playsuits, pajamas and sportswear. Rib knit bands are also used for garments made of non-stretch fabrics as wristbands, waistbands and neckbands. Rib knit can also be purchased in packaged quantities (called "ribbing") cut and finished to a specific length and width.

Unfortunately, rib knit fabric is not available in every fabric store. Keep asking for it and eventually the situation should improve now that it is becoming so popular. When I find rib knit fabric in inexpensive stores, I buy several colors in quantity. Some old knit sweaters or T-shirts might be used for rib knit bands. I have even bought a few new stretch nylon pullovers at sales, to cut into rib knit bands. Don't throw away old socks and kneehighs because usually only the sole is worn. Stretchy ankles and legs make excellent ribbing for sleeve and leg ends on children's T-shirts, pajamas and sportswear. The upper edge is non-raveling and doesn't even have to be folded. If the right side is worn and linty, check to see if the wrong side looks better. Before discarding old garments, check for any rib knit cuffs or waistbands in good shape for new use. If you can't find rib knit fabrics in stores, ask for any very stretchy fabric and you might find a good substitute.

To prepare a rib knit band to be sewn to the garment, cut a strip twice the desired finished length (here referring to the lengthwise grain) plus seam allowances, and as wide as desired (here referring to the stretchy crosswise grain) plus seam allowances. For a neat fit, the rib knit band is always cut somewhat shorter than the length of edge it is sewn to. Stitch band ends together from wrong side, forming a tube. Then fold the band in half (across stretchy width), wrong sides in and raw edges even (press lightly, if necessary, but without stretching the band). For a neckband or waistband, divide both the band and the garment's edge into four (or eight) equal sections and mark them with pins or tailor's chalk. It's not necessary to divide short edges such as cuffs or legbands. Turn the garment inside out including sleeve ends and leg ends. This is an easy and neat way to stitch rib knit bands around even the smallest sleeve ends (you don't put the sleeve ends around freearm). Pin the band inside (against the right side of garment), all raw edges even, matching marks. Place the band seam at neck center back, or at side seam of sleeves, legs, and waist. Rib knit band up against the presser foot and all raw edges even, stitch the band in place, stretching it as needed to straighten the garment's edge. Do not stretch the garment. Sew as you would sew any stretch fabric, i.e. by using ballpoint needle, polyester thread, and stretch stitch (or overlock or tiny zigzag).

When using a rib knit band around neck with front opening (jacket, coat), press the band in half right side out. Taper the front ends into rounded corners by pulling them down and cutting off the excess seam allowances. Band against the right side of garment and all raw edges even, pin the band around the neck and stitch it in place.

When sewing a rib knit band around the lower edge of a jacket with front opening, sew the band in place prior to stitching the zipper (sewing the zipper in place will close the band ends). If using buttons or snap fasteners instead of zipper closure, stitch band ends closed from wrong side prior to sewing the band around the lower edge of garment.

Instead of using rib knit fabric, you can make bands from self-fabric of a stretchy garment, or even from a different stretch fabric (maybe of contrasting color). Prepare the band and stitch it in place as described above. Neckband should be large enough, when stretched, for the head to fit through but not too large or it will look droopy. Generally speaking, you will not get as close-fitting bands from regular stretch fabrics as you will from rib knit, which combines stretch and close fit for a professional, neat look.

The seam joining the neckband to a stretch fabric T-shirt or pullover must be stretchy. If you only have a straight stitch machine and you wish to sew stretch fabrics, stitch the seam twice and stretch the fabric slightly as you sew. Add an opening with zipper, or button and loop, to the back of close-fitting, round neck opening, or choose a model with boat neck or V-neck.

Apart from rib knit bands, you can easily make many useful and comfortably warm items out of rib knit fabrics. Consider making tuques, balaclava helmets, tubular hoods (long enough to drape around neck), legwarmers, tank tops, extra-long wrists for mittens (to pull them over snowsuit sleeves), and sporty headbands. Use rib knit also for store-bought garments. Let's say you bought a nylon windbreaker for a child, and in no time it is too short. Cut off elasticized sleeve ends and cordstring casing from around the lower edge and extend the hem and sleeve ends with rib knit bands. If a hood is too loose or doesn't cover the forehead, sew a rib knit band around hood front edge, forming a casing, and insert a cord through it.

DECORATING GARMENTS WITH SEWING MACHINE

Decorating garments with your sewing machine can be fun and easy. This chapter gives you smart ideas on machine appliqués, machine embroidery, monograms and machine quilting, and on camouflaging accidents.

Use these methods to decorate children's clothes such as T-shirts, sweatshirts, vests, jackets, bibs and pockets of overalls and jumpers. Decorate adult garments of simple designs such as vests, jackets, capes, sweatshirts, T-shirts and kimonos. Garment sections are most conveniently decorated before stitching the seams.

For professional results, <u>loosen the top tension slightly</u> to ensure that bobbin thread or links will not be visible on the right side of garment. Lock the stitching lines at the beginning and end with a few <u>straight</u> stitches while the stitch length is in <u>zero</u> position.

When you have time and you are in a creative mood, make several appliqués for future use (by using "Ready-sewn method" described later). Then, when you need an appliqué, it will be a pleasure to select one from your stock and stitch it to the garment.

Make your own appliqués with either of these two easy methods ("Ready-sewn method" and "Fusing method"). After a little practice, they'll look just as good as store-bought ones.

Choosing the design and material for appliqués: Simple, bold designs are best. Trace patterns from magazines or children's books, or make your own. Experiment with a variety of fabric scraps with interesting textures such as Ultrasuede, velour, spandex, nylon, quilted fabrics, lace, lamés and sparkling fabrics, velveteen, fake fur, as well as regular cotton and polyester. Tightly woven fabrics are best. Add stability and body, if necessary, to limp or loosely-woven fabrics by ironing fusible interfacing to wrong side of appliqué materials. Remember that appliqué will be washed along with the garment so choose the material accordingly (preshrink if necessary).

Ready-sewn method: This method is practical and neat for appliqués consisting of one piece, or of separate pieces that are joined together or partially overlapped. You satin stitch the raw edges of the appliqué and add the details until the appliqué is completely finished, and only then do you stitch it to the garment. Cut the appliqué piece(s) out of desired fabric(s). Choose color(s) in contrast to the garment. If the design consists of several pieces, iron fusible interfacing to the wrong side to join the separate pieces together. Place a sheet of typing paper (or tear-away stabilizer such as Pellon) under the appliqué. Use embroidery foot. Cover all raw edges with satin stitch (wide, short zigzag). The typing paper (or tear-away stabilizer) helps you to stitch neatly

around edges and keeps the appliqué flat. Rip the paper (or stabilizer) off after you have finished sewing. Press the finished appliqué with steam iron. Stitch it to the garment with regular straight stitch (stitching along the inner edge of satin stitch will be least visible).

Fusing method: This method is convenient for large appliqués, or for appliqués with several non-joined pieces. Cut the appliqué piece(s) out of desired fabric(s). Bond the piece(s) to the garment by ironing with strips of fusible web between the appliqué and the garment. Place a sheet of typing paper (or tear-away stabilizer) underneath (between the garment and feed dogs), tear off after sewing. Use embroidery foot. Cover all raw edges of appliqué with satin stitch. Press.

Monograms: When sewing a monogram, trace the letter (or number) onto the fabric. For soft or stretch fabric, iron a piece of interfacing underneath, or slip a sheet of typing paper under the fabric. Use an embroidery hoop to keep fabric straight and taut (larger hoop on wrong side of work). Stitch the monogram with wide zigzag by dropping the feed control. Use darning foot and guide the work by hand without turning the fabric. Remember to lower the presser foot. Sew fast but move the hoop slowly so zigzag stitches will be very close together. Move the hoop faster when moving sideways. The finished monogram should be smooth and even. If it has gaps, sew a second run over the first one. Press with steam iron.

Monogramming is like writing with the needle. Experiment first on scrap fabric.

If your machine doesn't have a dropfeed control, use embroidery foot and stitch the monogram with regular satin stitch (sewing forward only), turning the fabric to follow the monogram lines.

To monogram fabric with nap or pile (such as corduroy, velour or terry) that wouldn't show tracing, trace the monogram on a sheet of typing paper. Position the fabric (with the paper on top) over the larger hoop and snap in the smaller ring (to keep both the fabric and the paper straight and taut). Stitch the monogram as above and tear the paper off after you have finished. Or, instead of paper, trace the design (backward) onto the wrong side of fabric, and hand-baste along the lines so that they show on right side.

Monogram garment prior to stitching the seams. Small items, such as a pocket, should be monogrammed prior to cutting the fabric. If you decide to monogram a pocket after you have already cut it out, baste pocket securely onto a larger piece of scrap fabric to enable you to use a hoop (trim excess scrap fabric off after you have finished).

Machine embroidery (outline method):
This easy method gives a beautiful decorative effect on a garment of a solid color. Use a drawing from a magazine or draw your own design on a sheet of paper, but don't cut it out. Iron interfacing under the fabric (or slip a sheet of typing paper or tear-away stabilizer underneath; rip it off after you have finished). Baste the entire drawing onto the garment with several vertical and horizontal lines to keep it securely in place. Use embroidery foot. Satin stitch all the lines of the drawing

with short, wide zigzag, using contrasting colored thread(s). After you have finished, rip off the drawing which is now broken where stitched through. The traces of paper left under stitches will wash away. Or, instead of satin stitch, stitch the drawing lines and details with free-motion straight stitch by dropping the feed dogs.

Machine embroidery (filling method):
Fill the above-mentioned outlined drawing entirely with free-motion zigzag or straight stitch in different colors. It's as if you would be darning a hole or, let's say, painting a picture. And, by the way, it is a smart way to camouflage a tear or hole. Use a darning foot (or no foot). Lower the feed dogs so you will be able to guide the fabric by hand in any direction (even backwards). Lower the presser foot lever. Before you start sewing, hold the thread ends taut to the back so they won't get drawn into the needleplate hole. Consider embroidering a nice design on a pocket, the bib of a child's jumpsuit or chef's apron, or on a kimono back.

Decorative satin stitch: To decorate
garments, you don't even need to use any specific design. Just a plain satin stitch in contrasting color forming a few stripes, curves, or whatever, across pockets, sleeve ends or bodice gives the garment that special, unique touch. No dropfeed control is necessary for this type of machine embroidery.

Machine quilting: This gives a lovely
touch to a garment. Quilt prior to sewing the seams. Baste a layer of quilt batting (or a layer or two of fleece or cotton knit fabric) between two layers of garment fabric (cut pattern parts to be quilted

double-layered). Topstitch multiple rows of straight or curvy lines (or "draw" a design with the machine needle) through all thicknesses.

For a repeat pattern (such as straight or curvy lines spaced at equal distance), make a template from self-adhesive vinyl; peel off the paper, stick vinyl onto fabric and stitch along (not through) edges; pull vinyl off and stick it in next position.

Quilting is suitable for garment parts that don't need to stretch. Use it for yokes, cuffs, belts, waistbands, neckbands of front-open jackets or V-neck pullovers. Consider this method also for decorating small parts of bodice front or back or sleeves of T-shirts, sweatshirts, dresses and jackets. Cut entire pockets double-layered for this purpose. Machine quilting looks good in velour, fleece, terry, cotton, nylon and silky fabrics.

Camouflage mistakes: Do it by something so smart it makes the accident a lucky one. I once burned the hem of a minidress, and covered the burn with patch pockets (decoratively topstitched) at the hemline. Sure enough, it was just the pockets, so unusually placed and decorated, that everyone admired. When a friend of mine mistakenly cut a blouse too narrow, she added a wide lace inset to side and underarm seams, and that made the blouse even more beautiful than the original design. Another friend burned the sleeve ends of a sheer blouse and covered the burns cleverly with rows of satin ribbons.

Let your own accidents challenge you to find perfect solutions to camouflage them!

SEWING IS MY HOBBY

I inherited my interest in sewing from my mother. It is thanks to her encouragement during my childhood in Finland that, for more than three decades now, I have found sewing to be such a source of pleasure, as well as an easy and enjoyable way of being creative. At times, sewing has even been an economical necessity.

Always interested in sewing or, let's say, easy sewing, I have tried to find shortcuts for quick yet beautiful results ever since I was six years old. My first attempts were disastrous. I reasoned that since dolls don't move, I could just as well baste the seams together and whip up a dozen garments, while my older sister labored with tiny stitches on the only dress she was able to finish in the meantime. I thought I was very smart -- until I tried dressing the dolls. All my beautiful creations fell apart. With that I learned the first important lesson in the art of sewing.

I still remember vividly how impressed I was to see my mother cut out a pair of panties for my doll without a pattern. Without realizing it then, I started storing in my mind the basics of pattern-making. My parents were farmers and we lived in the country far away from any good shopping facilities. Even if patterns had existed, country women found it more practical to make their own and share them with each other. The upper part of patterns were cut out of newspapers or brown wrapping paper "with a little short bit of upper bodice and a little short bit of upper sleeve" as my mother used to say. She used to draw the rest of the pattern herself according to the child's measurements.

That indeed was the only way of home sewing in the country because, back in the early 50's, commercial patterns for children were unavailable. I have three sisters, so it was practical to make dresses for all of us at the same time by just altering the pattern size slightly for each one. She encouraged us to use the sewing machine and bought lots of inexpensive fabrics so we could practice. I was ten years old when I made my first dress without a pattern. I can still remember how pretty it was when I wore it to school. That is how I got happily hooked on sewing.

I mention these early experiences in the hope that sewing mothers everywhere would share their talent with their children, to "teach them something worthwhile", as one of my readers so nicely put it. Encouragement does not mean proving how much better you are, but being there with a helping hand and lots of compliments. Many patterns in this book are so simple that even a ten year old child could sew them (perhaps with a little help from you).

At 15, I started sewing regularly and, due to my mother's style of sewing, it was natural to make my own patterns, although I used commercial patterns too. I now realize the talent and the patience my mother had, as well as the value of her teaching to last me a lifetime. Even if you didn't learn sewing from your own mother and have not had much experience in sewing, it is never too late to start. I hope this book will encourage you to realize that anyone can easily learn how to sew.

I have learned a lot since those early childhood days. Today sewing is my number one hobby, and for a good reason. While it saves money, it is also a rewarding occupation which gives quick results that can actually be worn immediately and get envious compliments from others. Unbelievable as it may sound, sewing can save time too. Just think of all the time spent shopping for ready-made clothes (often at rush-hour with tired children), trying them on, being frustrated by prices, shrinking garments, fixing poorly-made seams or rescuing loose buttons in time. At home, you can sew in comfort at any convenient time with this selection of basic patterns and an easy method of drawing new ones when necessary. Of course my sewing is now more than just a hobby since my dearest occupation has turned into the business that I subconsciously always wanted.

In these days sewing is easy and enjoyable thanks to good sewing machines, beautiful easy-care fabrics, and innumerable time-saving gadgets and notions to smooth away many frustrations.

Sewing for children can truly be a pleasure. It is very economical, not too complicated, it gives you a chance to be creative and use your imagination, and provides valuable experience for more serious and more complicated sewing projects. Furthermore, self-made children's clothes make wonderful gifts. I make most of my children's clothes at a savings of 60-90% as compared to ready-made clothing.

As a bonus, sewing keeps the children happily busy. They love the creative atmosphere around your sewing machine, and will be inspired to invent their own games to the theme. Children are resourceful enough to profit from almost any opportunity and will gradually collect many treasures among the empty spools, material scraps, ribbons and pretty buttons.

Still a fan of quick sewing, I am always searching for new ideas on easy and enjoyable shortcuts, while over the years I have developed many of my own. I am happy to share them with you through this book.

CREATE YOUR OWN DESIGNS

This collection of basic patterns provides you with an endless source of versatile, timeless designs, that are simple to sew. Use them as a guide to create your own styles which reflect your personal needs and tastes.

Leaf through all designs and directions and you might find useful tips and ideas in them, even if you don't use some patterns "as is".

Pull-on pants and shorts designed without side seams can be trimmed down sides with contrasting stripes or tapes for a sporty look. Or, for mock cording, place the cord along leg's side-fold on wrong side of fabric. Fold fabric over cord and topstitch from the right side through both thicknesses with zipper foot close to covered cord, encasing it tightly. Or, cut the pattern apart at sides from waist to hem, add seam allowances, and stitch piping (from bias tape) between seams.

I have mentioned variations for some of these patterns. Pull-on pants with sweatshirt can be unisex pajamas or sportswear. Cut a T-shirt longer for a dress or nightgown. A jacket can also become a coat or bathrobe. With a pattern for pull-on pants, cutting lines allow you to make shorts too.

Once you get used to it, it is easier to manipulate a miniature pattern than a full-size one. Try changing my patterns or designing a few of your own on any paper with small squares. Once it "looks" right, enlarge it (recheck the measurements at this point before cutting out the fabric) and sew it, and you might well have discovered a rewarding, hidden talent that will continue to give you creative pleasure in the future.

An easy way to start designing your own patterns is to use a basic pattern as a guide, and add your own touch to it. Take a sleeveless top and add a gathered ruffle from self-fabric or different fabric to make a lovely summer dress. Take a maillot, make it a bodysuit, add sleeves if desired, add a little ruffled skirt below waist, and make it a skating or gym suit. Take a T-shirt, add a ruffle or ruffled lace between sleeves and bodice and lengthen it for a nightgown. Or take a simple, favorite garment such as a T-shirt or pajamas that your child has outgrown, and try making a pattern from it, lengthening it at the same time. You don't even need to cut the original garment apart to make a pattern. Just place the old garment, appropriately folded, directly onto the fabric, add some extra plus seam allowances, and cut it out. Or, measure the old garment for all necessary measurements, add some extra plus seam allowances, and draw a new pattern.

Once you have enlarged a pattern, let it inspire you to create a unique, new design. Cut it apart any way you like, vertically, horizontally or on the bias. Add seam allowances to all newly-made seams. Cut the separate pieces out of complimentary colors, or out of different fabrics, or add piping trim in between. This is especially easy and attractive for T-shirts and sweatshirts, maillots and swimtrunks.

Start your own fashion scrapbook. Whenever you see something you like in magazine articles and advertisements, at stores, or on TV, cut it out or make a simple sketch so you won't forget it. Then go through the patterns in this book to see if any of them could be used "as is", enlarged or reduced, combined, or adapted to sew that garment.

Good ideas are there all around you. All you have to do is to realize that you can easily create the same or even better designs and sew them yourself. You will be so happy and proud of yourself, that you might want to order some labels (original by...) to attach to garments you have sewn. You'll find such labels by mail-order advertised in sewing magazines or they can be ordered through some fabric stores.

EASY WEAR AND CARE

Everyday clothes for children should be made with easy-care fabrics, so they can be machine washed and dried. These clothes must withstand repeated washings and should be easy to put on and take off.

To encourage children to dress themselves, mark the back of pull-on pants, T-shirts, sweatshirts, and pull-on skirts (when the back and front are so similar that it is difficult to tell them apart) with a piece of ribbon, tape or yarn stitched to the inside of waistband or neckband.

When using a drawstring cord through waist or hood casing, prevent it from slipping out by catching the cord to the casing at waist center back and hood center top with a few stitches. This is a practical tip also for store-bought garments.

To add extra strength to garments sewn with straight stitch, stitch seams like crotch and armholes twice. Stretch stitch is more durable than straight stitch, so double stitching is not necessary. Sew buttons very securely with buttonhole twist thread or dental floss. Use fusible web for quick hems if you don't use topstitching, which usually is the fastest and the most durable way to hem children's clothes. Add patches to pants' knees prior to sewing side seams. Cut the patches as wide as the pants, stitch upper and lower edges securely to the wrong side of the garment, and stitch patch sides together with side seams and inner leg seams.

When washing garments, close all zippers, open buttons and empty pockets (brush them out if necessary). To keep them looking great longer, all garments (but especially those made of fabrics with nap, such as velour and corduroy) should be turned inside out. That way they don't spread their lint to other items in the wash, or attract lint from other items that may stick to their nap.

Today's easy-care fabrics and lifestyle almost prohibit the use of an iron. However, a good steam iron nowadays is so light and easy to use, and gives such a lovely, almost luxurious feeling to clothes that, from time to time, I find myself actually enjoying a little ironing just to touch up. Perhaps the beautiful smell of clean, freshly ironed laundry brings back nostalgic childhood memories that I want to pass on to my own children.

SEWING FOR ALLERGIC CHILDREN

If you sew for an allergic child with a sensitive skin, use these tips for comfort.

Neckbands, sleeves and waistbands should not be too tight to cause irritation. Seams should be narrow and neat, not bulky, and the design should have sufficient ease for free, unrestricted movements. Elastic should be encased and of soft, non-binding quality, and never too tight. Design clothes without zippers or so that the metal part of zipper will not touch the skin.

Synthetic fibers may cause allergic itching. The best fabrics for an allergic child are made of 100% cotton which gets softer and even more comfortable after repeated washings. Excessively warm and thick clothing can cause perspiring, itching and discomfort. An allergic child's clothes (or fabrics prior to sewing) should be washed well, before wearing for the first time, to remove all traces of coloring and finishing agents, that may irritate the skin. Improper rinsing and fabric softeners may also cause irritation for an allergic child.

EXTENDING GARMENT LIFE

Tips for extending garment life are mentioned for some of the designs in this book. Since my style of sewing is so fast and inexpensive, I usually prefer making a brand new garment rather than spending hours on complicated and frustrating alterations to make a garment longer and larger. I have, however, a few favorite, fast tips for extending garment life that you might find useful.

The easiest way to lengthen the dress or skirt, without unstitching the hem, is by stitching a ruffle or eyelet edge around the hem. Or cut all around the hem about 5cm (2") from the lower edge and spread apart by sewing an eyelet or lace insert between.

Pants are designed with straight legs so that, if legs are too long or if you wish to cut them even longer, they are easy and neat just to fold up. (Consider lining lower ends with suitable fabric since they will show when turned up.)

Many of these patterns are designed with raglan or dolman sleeves, or are sleeveless, and made from stretch fabrics for built-in room for growth.

Cut straps for overalls extra long to lengthen them easily by changing the button positions.

If you cut skirts, pants or sleeves with a wide hem allowance to let out later, and the originally folded edge looks faded from wear and washings, conceal it with ribbon or decorative tape or rows of lace, or go over it with permanent marker of matching color.

Cut pull-on pants long enough to use elasticized leg ends. Lengthen the pants later by cutting off the elasticized edges (don't bother undoing the casing) and replacing them with rib knit bands.

For a preschooler, you can use rib knit bands even for overalls and jeans when they become too short. Instead of rib knit, velour works well, too, especially for corduroy pants. The pants will look so smart and will be so warm and convenient with boots, that you can't wait for other pants to get short too. You might even want to cut some pants off just below knees and add long, narrow rib knit bands that extend all the way down to ankles.

You can lengthen overalls or coveralls by cutting the garment apart at waist (rip zipper out temporarily below cut), stitch rib knit or any suitable fabric around waist between the pieces that are cut apart, and stitch lower part of the zipper back in new position. Or make pull-on pants out of them.

Add width to garments by stitching decorative fabric strips between side seams, raglan seams, and underarms of sleeve seams.

When you want to make pull-on pants or pull-on skirts out of old garments and don't have enough fabric for self-encased elastic at waist, stitch on decorative wide elastic for a waistband.

When long sleeves become too short, make them short sleeves. A too-short dress can be cut off at underarms to make a skirt with elasticized waist.

When cotton knit pajamas become too short, cut the sleeves and legs shorter. (My son actually prefers them to long pajamas and wants me to sew them short right from the beginning.)

When a coat becomes too short, make it a jacket. Extend sleeves with rib knit bands, cut lower edge at hips and add rib knit waistband.

When a ruffled sundress with shirred upper edge becomes too short, remove the straps and use it as a skirt with shirred upper edge as a waistband.

Certain designs, such as long nightgowns or T-shirtdresses, gradually get shorter while being usable all the time without any effort on your part, the long nightgown becoming a short one, and the T-shirtdress becoming a hip-length blouson and finally a T-shirt.

If a T-shirt is too tight across shoulders, make it a tank top. Cut sleeves off completely, enlarge armholes and neckhole, add doublefold stretch tape or rib knit bands.

If a jacket (corduroy, denim, quilted fabrics) becomes too tight and short, take the sleeves off, and make it a vest. Add rib knit bands to armholes.

Cut jeans short or knee-length, or extend the legs with bands of contrasting fabric (band as wide as the leg ends), and use matching fabric to decorate the jeans with appliqués. You might even like to make a matching vest.

Use the above-mentioned tips also for store-bought clothes. Let every garment inspire you to invent more extension tips to suit the child's needs.

MADE TO MEASURE

Draw your child's outline on a sheet of paper or cardboard, so you can refer to it for sleeve and pants' length, even if the child is sleeping, away, or so squirmy when you sew that you can't try the garment on. Also mention all the important measurements of your child on the paper but remember that children grow very fast and you need new measurements frequently.

If it is impractical to draw the child's outline on a paper, record the measurements at least every six months. A garment of currently suitable size for your child can solve many of your measuring problems when sewing.

PATTERNS

Commercial patterns are well-made with professional and detailed instructions. I have a good collection of them and I subscribe to several home sewing pattern magazines for inspiration and up-to-date fashion information. I have also created my own collection of basic patterns, and have learned to change them for several variations.

When I did not find the patterns I wanted for infants, I made my own. Thereafter, it was natural to continue making patterns for older children and adults too. It can be surprisingly easy, providing you have the time, some patience, and lots of inexpensive fabric for testing. Once you get more experienced in sewing and pattern-making, you gain confidence and will be able to duplicate the garments you find in stores, even to improve upon them.

This book contains seventy-five of my favorite patterns for 3-10 year-old children. Many of these patterns have been inspired by garments that have become favorites among those bought, received or made for my own children and for friends and relatives. Sometimes I see garments I like in magazines and boutiques or on children passing by. I sketch what I like and make my own pattern and, at the same time, usually change and simplify the design. I have created many patterns especially for this book, choosing really simple basic designs with as few details and pattern pieces as possible. Many of the patterns are unisex. T-shirts, shorts, sportswear, jackets, pajamas, and many other practical garments can be worn by both boys and girls.

One of my favorite letters is from a mother who found my easy patterns a blessing after being frustrated by commercial patterns for children that "are so complicated and with so many pattern pieces that only somebody without children would have time to make them". I sincerely hope that you will find my patterns easy enough to encourage you to take the time to sew them.

All patterns have been tested to be sure they are easy enough to earn a place in this book. Simple, yet detailed line drawings allow you to see the potential value and versatility of each pattern. While sewing them, I was constantly thinking of shortcuts and taking notes in order to give you the simplest possible method.

Easy to enlarge and easy to sew, my patterns will save you lots of good money and help you in creating practical, comfortable and beautiful clothes for children.

SIMPLE PATTERN ADJUSTMENTS

Compare the measurements of the child with the pattern, particularly sleeve length, garment length and width. If necessary, adjust the pattern size prior to cutting out the fabric. When convenient, make adjustments when enlarging the miniature pattern to full size. Use this simple method also to change pattern size to fit your child, if you are using designs from another age group.

To enlarge

Cut the pattern apart vertically and horizontally at several points. Spread the pieces apart until desired size is achieved. Slip a piece of paper underneath and tape it in place to bridge the separated pieces together. When enlarging a garment with sleeves, enlarge the sleeves as well to match the new, larger armhole. Draw the new outline.

To reduce

Pleat the pattern vertically and horizontally at several points until desired size is achieved. Tape the pleats in place. Or use pins so that you can easily remove them later, if you want to use the larger size when your child has grown into it.

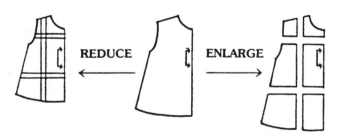

REDUCE ← → ENLARGE

PATTERN SIZES

This book contains patterns fitting children from three to ten years old. Sizing was not easy because children's measurements differ so much. Therefore it's impossible to make patterns that would fit absolutely everybody in the same age group without any adjustments.

I sized these patterns generously for average to taller-than-average children of medium frame, with sufficient ease for proper fit and comfort. If you like shorter garments, simply cut the pattern shorter. Handy tips on extending garment life are mentioned for some of the patterns.

If your child is much taller/shorter or chubbier/slimmer than mentioned below, enlarge/reduce pattern size prior to cutting out the fabric. When convenient, make the adjustments when enlarging the pattern to full size. You might also choose designs for younger or older children if their measurements are closer to your child's measurements.

Child's age in years	3	4	6	8	10
	cm/in	cm/in	cm/in	cm/in	cm/in
Height (up to)	94(37)	102(40)	119(47)	132(52)	142(56)
Chest	56(22)	58(23)	64(25)	68(27)	72(28½)
Waist	52(20½)	53(21)	56(22)	60(23½)	62(24½)
Hips	58(23)	61(24)	66(26)	71(28)	76(30)
Pants side seam	56(22)	61(24)	71(28)	81(32)	86(34)
Pants inseam	37(14½)	41(16)	51(20)	61(24)	66(26)
Long sleeve length	33(13)	38(15)	41(16)	43(17)	47(18½)

SEAM ALLOWANCES

Adult garments look good with narrow well-finished seam allowances. To avoid bulk, the seam allowances of infants' and children's clothes should also be narrow. The children grow mostly lengthwise and hardly at all in width, so I don't find it practical to use large seam allowances for growing-room except in length.

The patterns in my books INCLUDE the following seam and hem allowances (unless otherwise indicated):

Infants: 6mm (1/4") for seams, and 2½cm (1") for hem.
Children: 1cm (3/8") for seams and 2½-5cm (1-2") for hem.
Adults: 1cm (3/8") for seams and 2½cm (1") for hem. (Lengthen or shorten the pattern, if necessary, prior to cutting out the fabric.)

MARKS USED IN PATTERNS

Cutting line.

Place the pattern on fold of fabric. DO NOT CUT ON THIS LINE. (Fold always on lengthwise straight grain, except when on the bias, or otherwise indicated.)

Gather. (Sew two rows of long stitches close to each other, and pull the bobbin threads to distribute fullness evenly into gathers.)

Folding line (or side line; or edge for pockets, facings, crotch).

Place on straight lengthwise grain.

Buttons, buttonholes.

1 2 3 4   Match same numbers when sewing.

PATTERNS AND INSTRUCTIONS

1. DRESS (or nightgown)
2. PANTIES
Size: 3

Ruffle around lower edge and puffed sleeves of contrasting color. Close-fitting panties. (Eliminate ruffle for nightgown.)

Stretch fabrics only: Cotton knits, velour, stretch terry. **Fabric required:** Dress and panties – 60x115cm (2/3ydx45"); contrasting fabric for sleeves, ruffle, panties' legbands – 30x115cm (1/3ydx45"). **Notions:** Narrow elastic for sleeve ends, wide elastic for panties.

Sewing dress: Sew an appliqué onto front. Stitch left shoulder seam. Bind neck opening with bifold stretch tape made of self fabric (see page 35). Stitch right shoulder seam. Gather sleeve tops and stitch them to armholes. Stitch sides and underarms. Overlock sleeve ends, stitch them down into narrow casings, insert elastic. Stitch ruffle ends together into a circle, hem lower edge narrowly, gather upper edge and stitch it around lower edge of dress.

Sewing panties: Stitch side seams. Stitch each legband into a circle, press in half lengthwise, wrong sides together and raw edges even. Turn panties inside out and stitch the bands around legholes, stretching slightly. Sew waist edge down to form casing and insert elastic.

3. DRESS
Size: 3

Raglan sleeves, front and back yoke, separating front zipper. Make matching panties #2. (When too short, wear as a top next year, and make matching pull-on pants with pattern #25.)

Stretch fabrics only: Velour, cotton knits, stretch terry. **Fabric required:** Dress, sleeves, neckband and panties – 120x115cm (1 1/4 ydx45"); contrasting fabric for yoke, sleevebands, panties' legbands – 25x115cm (10x45"). **Notions:** 35cm (14") long separating zipper, elastic for panties' waist.

Sewing dress: Stitch sleeves to armhole edges of front and back. Stitch shoulder seams of yoke. Stitch yoke to garment and to sleeves in one continuous seam. Stitch sides and underarms. Sew zipper in place. (Or, instead of a separating zipper, use a shorter regular one, and stitch the front seam closed below the zipper.) Stitch each sleeveband into a circle, press in half wrong sides together and raw edges even, turn sleeves inside out and stitch the bands around sleeve ends. Fold neckband in half right sides together, stitch ends closed, turn right side out and press, stitch the band around neck opening. Overlock lower edge of dress, press it under and topstitch in place.

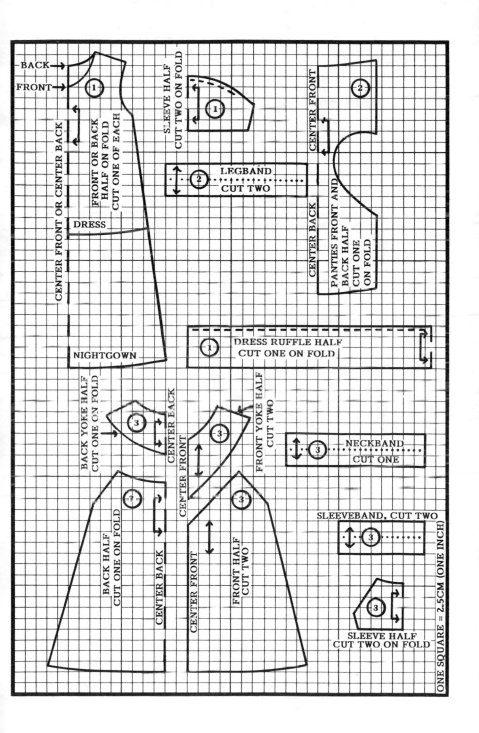

BACK →
FRONT →

CENTER FRONT OR CENTER BACK

FRONT OR BACK HALF ON FOLD
CUT ONE OF EACH

DRESS

NIGHTGOWN

SLEEVE HALF
CUT TWO ON FOLD

①

② LEGBAND
CUT TWO

CENTER FRONT

②

CENTER BACK

PANTIES FRONT AND
BACK HALF
CUT ONE
ON FOLD

① DRESS RUFFLE HALF
CUT ONE ON FOLD

BACK YOKE HALF
CUT ONE ON FOLD

CENTER BACK

③

CENTER FRONT

③

FRONT YOKE HALF
CUT TWO

③ NECKBAND
CUT ONE

BACK HALF
CUT ONE ON FOLD

CENTER BACK

CENTER FRONT

FRONT HALF
CUT TWO

③

SLEEVEBAND, CUT TWO

③

SLEEVE HALF
CUT TWO ON FOLD

③

ONE SQUARE = 2.5CM (ONE INCH)

61

4. JUMPSUIT OR KNICKERS
Size: 3

<u>Jumpsuit:</u> Shirred upper edge, shoulder straps, self-ruffled leg ends. <u>Knickers:</u> Elasticized waist, knee side-slits, legs gathered to kneebands extending into self ties.
Suggested fabrics: Lightweight cotton types, calico, eyelet, broadcloth, seersucker, cotton knits. (Knickers: Also velour, fleece.) **Fabric required:** Jumpsuit – 1mx115cm (1ydx45"); knickers – 70x115cm (3/4ydx45"). **Notions:** Jumpsuit – Elastic thread for shirring. Knickers – Elastic, bias tape.

<u>Sewing jumpsuit:</u> Stitch center front seam. Narrowly hem upper edge and leg ends. Stitch several rows of elastic shirring across upper edge, and at ankles 5cm (2") up from leg ends forming self ruffles (page 33). Stitch center back seam and inner leg seams. Stitch rows of shirring along shoulder straps. Fold the straps in half lengthwise, stitch sides, turn right side out. Stitch straps in place.
<u>Sewing knickers:</u> Cut 8cm (3") long slits at knee sides, bind slit edges with doublefold bias tape. Stitch inner leg seams. Stitch center front and center back seams. Stitch waist edge down into a casing, insert elastic. Gather leg ends. Press kneebands doublefold, stitch them around knees (edgestitch tie-ends).

5. T-SHIRT (or dress, nightgown)
Size: 3

Short raglan sleeves, round neck opening with rib knit band. (Lengthen the pattern for dress or nightgown.)
Stretch fabrics only: Cotton knits, stretch terry, velour. **Fabric required:** 60x90cm (2/3ydx36"). **Notions:** Rib knit.

<u>Sewing:</u> Stitch sleeves to armhole edges of front and back. Stitch sides and underarms. Overlock hem and sleeve ends, press them under and topstitch in place. Stitch rib knit band around neck.

6. HOODED TOP
Size: 3

Short sleeves, drawstring hood, kangaroo pockets.
Stretch fabrics only: Cotton knits, velour, stretch terry. **Fabric required:** 70x115cm (3/4ydx45"). **Notions:** 100cm (40") long cord.

<u>Sewing:</u> Overlock bias edge of each pocket, topstitch them down, press upper edges under and topstitch pockets in place. Stitch center front seam, leaving 10cm (4") open at neck. Stitch shoulder seams. Make buttonholes in hood facing allowances as shown in the pattern. Stitch hood center seam. Stitch hood to neck edge. Stitch the front edges of hood and front opening under. Stitch sleeves to armholes. Stitch sides and underarms. Press under and topstitch in place 5cm (2") from sleeve ends and 2.5cm (1") from lower edge. Turn up a 2.5cm (1") cuff on each sleeve, topstitch folded edge in place. Insert a cord through hood casing.

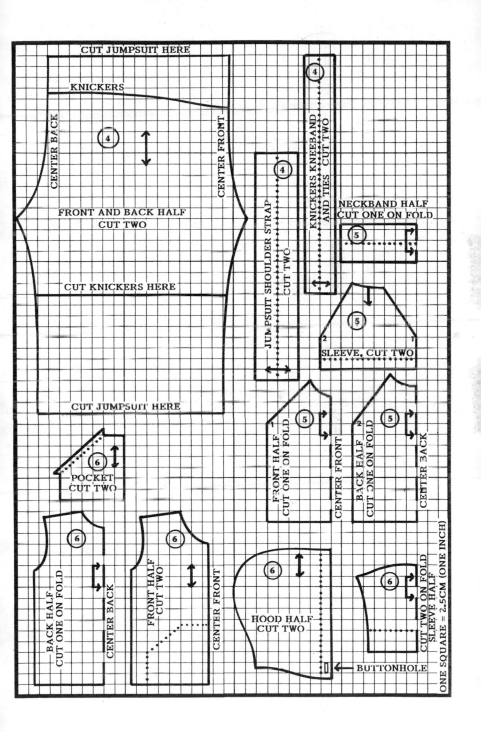

CUT JUMPSUIT HERE

KNICKERS

CENTER BACK

④

FRONT AND BACK HALF
CUT TWO

CENTER FRONT

CUT KNICKERS HERE

CUT JUMPSUIT HERE

④ KNICKERS KNEEBAND
AND TIES CUT TWO

④ JUMPSUIT SHOULDER STRAP
CUT TWO

NECKBAND HALF
CUT ONE ON FOLD

⑤

⑤

2   SLEEVE, CUT TWO   1

⑥ POCKET
CUT TWO

⑤ FRONT HALF
CUT ONE ON FOLD

CENTER FRONT

⑤ BACK HALF
CUT ONE ON FOLD

CENTER BACK

⑥ BACK HALF
CUT ONE ON FOLD

CENTER BACK

⑥ FRONT HALF
CUT TWO

CENTER FRONT

⑥ HOOD HALF
CUT TWO

⑥ CUT TWO ON FOLD
SLEEVE HALF

BUTTONHOLE

ONE SQUARE = 2.5CM (ONE INCH)

63

7. JUMPER
Size: 3

Loose-fitting design, straps buttoned to frontband. (When too short, make it a skirt, add waistband and elastic suspenders.)
Suggested fabrics: Pinwale corduroy, mediumweight cotton types, quilted fabrics, velour, fleece. **Fabric required:** 1mx115cm (1ydx45"). **Notions:** Two buttons.

Sewing: Stitch side seams. Overlock underarms, press them under and topstitch in place. Fold frontband in half lengthwise, stitch ends closed, turn right side out and press. Stitch the two strap layers together, clip curves, turn right side out and press. Pleat upper edge of skirt front and stitch it to frontband. Pleat upper edge of skirt back and stitch it to straps. Add buttons and buttonholes. Overlock lower edge and topstitch it under.

8. PULLOVER (or dress, nightgown)
Size: 3

Loose-fitting turtleneck with short or long sleeves. (Knee-length dress or nightgown, round neck opening with self stretch binding; see #1. Dress has elasticized waist.)
Stretch fabrics only: Cotton knits, stretch terry, velour. **Fabric required:** 50x115cm (½ydx45").

Sewing: Stitch shoulder seams. Stitch sleeves to armholes. Stitch sides and underarms. Overlock sleeve ends and lower edge, press them under and topstitch in place. Turn the garment inside out. Stitch collar ends together into a tube, fold the collar in half wrong sides together and stitch it around neck.

9. JACKET (or coat, bathrobe, vest)
Size: 3

Loose-fitting straight jacket with rib knit neckband, patch pockets, button closure. (When too short, lengthen jacket sleeves and lower edge with rib knit bands. Make a vest with jacket pattern by leaving sleeves off, trim armholes with rib knit bands.)
Suggested fabrics: Lightweight corduroy or mediumweight cotton types. (Terry or stretch terry for bathrobe.) **Fabric required:** 1mx115cm (1ydx45"). **Notions:** Five buttons, rib knit for neckband, doublefold bias tape.

Sewing: Sew bias tape all around pockets, topstitch pockets in place. Stitch shoulder seams. Stitch sleeves to armholes. Stitch sides and underarms. Overlock front edges and press them under. Stitch rib knit band around neck. Overlock sleeve ends and lower edge, press them under and topstitch in place. Make buttonholes and sew on buttons.

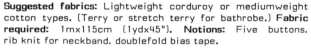

Save the elastic waistbands from worn pantyhose and use them for children's clothes.

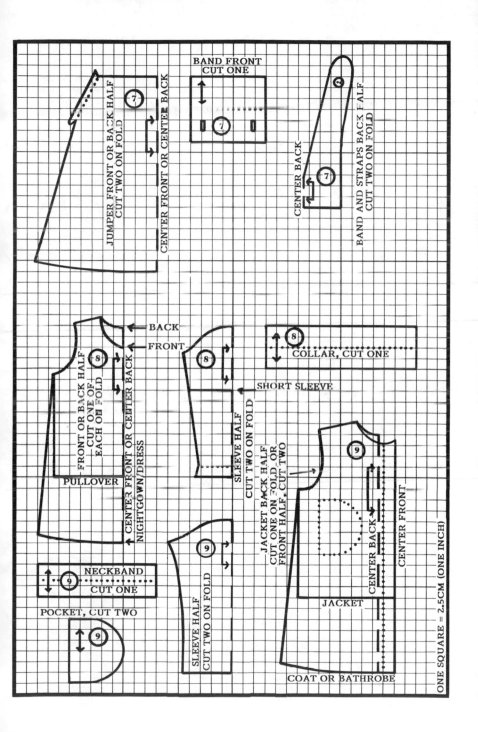

BAND FRONT
CUT ONE

⑦

JUMPER FRONT OR BACK HALF
CUT TWO ON FOLD

CENTER FRONT OR CENTER BACK

⑦

CENTER BACK

BAND AND STRAPS BACK HALF
CUT TWO ON FOLD

⑦

← BACK

← FRONT

⑧

COLLAR, CUT ONE

⑧

SHORT SLEEVE

FRONT OR BACK HALF
CUT ONE OF
EACH ON FOLD

CENTER FRONT OR CENTER BACK
NIGHTGOWN/DRESS

PULLOVER

⑧

SLEEVE HALF
CUT TWO ON FOLD

⑨

JACKET BACK HALF
CUT ONE ON FOLD, OR
FRONT HALF, CUT TWO

CENTER BACK

CENTER FRONT

JACKET

⑨

NECKBAND
CUT ONE

POCKET, CUT TWO

⑨

SLEEVE HALF
CUT TWO ON FOLD

⑨

COAT OR BATHROBE

ONE SQUARE = 2.5CM (ONE INCH)

10. COVERALLS (shorts, pull-on pants)
Size: 3

Long or short sleeves, front zipper, rib knit bands around neck and sleeve ends, patch pockets, no side seams. Optional elasticized waist. Or eliminate sleeves and trim armholes with rib knit bands. (When too short, make pull-on pants with elasticized waist. Lengthen leg ends with rib knit bands.)

Suggested fabrics: Stretch terry, velour, mediumweight cotton knits, fleece, cotton types. **Fabric required:** 140x115cm (1½ydx45"). **Notions:** 25cm (10") long zipper, elastic for waist, rib knit for sleevebands and neckband.

Sewing: Prepare pockets and topstitch them in place. Sew zipper in place. Stitch center front seam below zipper. Stitch center back seam. Stitch inner leg seams. Stitch shoulder seams. Stitch underarm seams of sleeves. Stitch sleeves to armholes. Stitch rib knit bands around sleeve ends and neck. Overlock leg ends, press them under and topstitch in place. If desired, stitch stretched elastic around waist on the wrong side of fabric. (Sew pants and shorts as for design #54.)

11. TANK TOP (or dress, nightgown)
Size: 3

Sleeveless top with self stretch binding around armholes and neck. (Or sew rib knit bands to armholes, neck and hem. Add ruffle around hem for a minidress, make matching panties with pattern #2. Lengthen pattern for nightie.)
Stretch fabrics only: Cotton knits, stretch terry, velour, rib knit. (Enlarge pattern if you wish to use non-stretch mesh fabric.) **Fabric required:** 50x90cm (½ydx36"), makes two tops.

Sewing: Stitch left shoulder seam. Bind raw neck edge with bifold stretch tape made of self fabric or contrasting fabric (see page 35). Stitch right shoulder seam. Bind raw armholes with bifold stretch tape. Stitch side seams. Overlock lower edge, press it under and topstitch in place.

Reduce lint by turning garments inside out for laundering.

Need fabric strips for bias or stretchy tapes? Cut the strip first from self-adhesive vinyl, peel off the paper, stick vinyl onto fabric, and cut along the edges. Pull vinyl off and reuse it. No marking, folding or pins. Fabric won't slide or stretch.

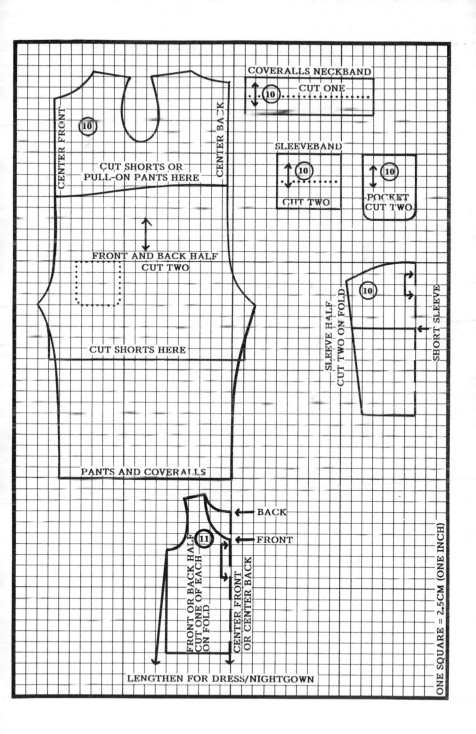

CENTER FRONT

⑩

CUT SHORTS OR
PULL-ON PANTS HERE

CENTER BACK

FRONT AND BACK HALF
CUT TWO

CUT SHORTS HERE

PANTS AND COVERALLS

COVERALLS NECKBAND
⑩ ..... CUT ONE

SLEEVEBAND
⑩ .....
CUT TWO

⑩
POCKET
CUT TWO

⑩
SLEEVE HALF
CUT TWO ON FOLD

SHORT SLEEVE

BACK
⑪ FRONT

FRONT OR BACK HALF
CUT ONE OF EACH
ON FOLD

CENTER FRONT
OR CENTER BACK

ONE SQUARE = 2.5CM (ONE INCH)

LENGTHEN FOR DRESS/NIGHTGOWN

67

12. NIGHTGOWN (or blouse, dress)
Size: 3

Loose-fitting nightgown, short or long raglan sleeves, elasticized neck opening and sleeve ends. (Shorten pattern for blouse or dress. Dress, made of velour or fleece, has rib knit bands around gathered neck opening and gathered sleeve ends. Lightweight cotton knit blouse has eyelet trim around sleeve ends and neck opening, elasticized waist.)

Suggested fabrics: Lightweight cotton types, seersucker, flannelette, batiste, cotton knits. Flame-retardant fabrics are required by law on children's sleepwear. (Velour or fleece for dress.) **Fabric required:** 140x115cm (1½ydx45"). **Notions:** Narrow elastic for sleeve ends and neck opening. (Rib knit for dress neckband and sleevebands. Eyelet ribbon for blouse neck opening and sleeve ends.)

Sewing: Stitch sleeves to armhole edges of front and back. Stitch sides and underarms. Hem sleeve ends and neck edge narrowly. On inside, stitch stretched elastic about 2.5cm (1") from sleeve ends and neck edges, forming self ruffles. Hem lower edge. If your home has stairs or your child sleeps in a bunk-bed, cut nightgown shorter so that the child will not trip over.

13. DOLMAN TOP (dress, nightgown)
Size: 3

Boat neck, shoulders extend into 3/4-sleeves (roll them up if desired). (Add ruffle around lower edge for a dress. Lengthen the pattern for nightgown.)
Stretch fabrics only: Cotton knits, stretch terry, velour. **Fabric required:** 50x140cm (½ydx55").

Sewing: Stitch shoulder seams. Stitch neck facings together into a circle, overlock outer edge, stitch the facing around neck, press it to inside and topstitch in place. Stitch sides and underarms. Stitch bands to sleeve ends. Overlock lower edge, press it under and topstitch in place.

Don't fold fusible interfacing or webbing; roll up leftover pieces into empty cardboard tubes from paper towels, aluminum foil, etc.

Toddlers will give you sewing peace if you let them 'sew', too. Give the child a narrow shoe lace to thread through plastic canvas.

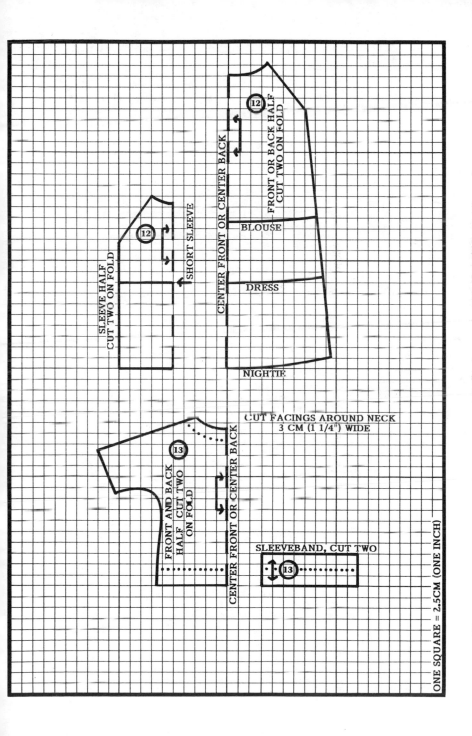

SLEEVE HALF —CUT TWO ON FOLD

SHORT SLEEVE

CENTER FRONT OR CENTER BACK

FRONT OR BACK HALF CUT TWO ON FOLD

BLOUSE

DRESS

NIGHTIE

CUT FACINGS AROUND NECK 3 CM (1 1/4") WIDE

FRONT AND BACK HALF CUT TWO ON FOLD

CENTER FRONT OR CENTER BACK

SLEEVEBAND, CUT TWO

ONE SQUARE = 2.5CM (ONE INCH)

14. OVERALLS (shorts, pull-on pants)
Size: 3

Loose-fitting, straight overalls, straps with buttons, patch pockets. (When too short, lengthen leg ends with rib knit bands. Later you can make them into pull-on pants and then into shorts.)
Suggested fabrics: Corduroy, soft denim, mediumweight cotton types, fleece, quilted fabrics, windproof and water repellent fabrics. **Fabric required:** 140x115cm (1½ydx45"). **Notions:** Two buttons.

Sewing: Stitch center front seam. Prepare pockets and stitch them in place. Sew an appliqué onto front if desired. Stitch center front seam of facing (unless cut on the fold). Stitch facing to garment around all upper edges and shoulder straps, trim corners and clip curves, turn right side out and press. Stitch center back seam of pants and facing. Turn facing to inside and topstitch it in place around entire upper edge. Catch facing in place under arms with vertical topstitching. Stitch inner leg seams. Make buttonholes and sew on buttons. Overlock leg ends, press them under and topstitch in place. (If you use quilted fabric, trim raw upper edges and shoulder straps with extra-wide doublefold bias tape instead of a facing.)

15. CAP
Size: 3

Easy cap with brim, elasticized back. (Optional ear warmer piece attached under chin with button or snap.)
Suggested fabrics: Mediumweight cotton types, denim, corduroy, quilted fabrics. **Fabric required:** 25x115cm (1/4ydx45"). (Extra fabric required for ear warmer.) **Notions:** Fusible interfacing, elastic.

Sewing: Iron fusible interfacing to wrong side of one brim. Stitch brims together around outer edge, clip curves, turn right side out and press. Topstitch around outer edge. Stitch the four crown sections together. Stitch brim to crown. Stitch facing ends together into a circle, overlock outer edge. Right sides together, all raw edges even and brim in between, stitch the facing to lower edge of crown. Stitch a 8cm (3") piece of elastic to the back edge seam allowance, stretching the elastic to its maximum length while sewing. Turn facing to inside and topstitch it in place around crown's lower edge. (Optional ear warmer: Stitch sides and lower edge, trim curves, turn right side out and press. Stitch the earwarmer in place under crown's edge. Add button/buttonhole or snap or a piece of Velcro.)

With fusible web, iron soft fleece between the two layers of fabric that you wish to quilt.

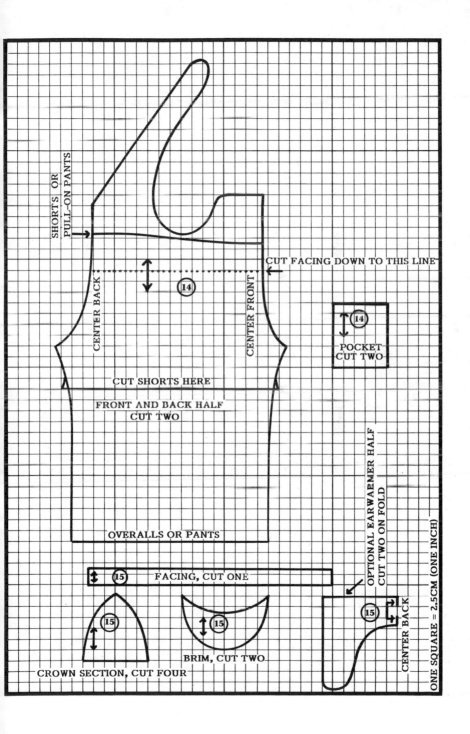

SHORTS OR PULL-ON PANTS

CENTER BACK

CUT FACING DOWN TO THIS LINE

⑭

CENTER FRONT

⑭

POCKET
CUT TWO

CUT SHORTS HERE

FRONT AND BACK HALF
CUT TWO

OPTIONAL EARWARMER HALF
CUT TWO ON FOLD

OVERALLS OR PANTS

⑮ FACING, CUT ONE

⑮

⑮

CENTER BACK

⑮

CROWN SECTION, CUT FOUR

BRIM, CUT TWO

ONE SQUARE = 2.5CM (ONE INCH)

71

16. JUMPSUIT
Size: 4

Loose-fitting design with straight legs, no side seams. Pleated front and back, straps buttoned to frontband. Optional patch pockets. (When too short, extend leg ends with rib knit bands. When straps become too short, cut them off and make pull-on pants or shorts with elasticized waist.)

Suggested fabrics: Corduroy, soft denim, mediumweight cotton types, fleece. **Fabric required:** 120x115cm (1 1/3 ydx45"). **Notions:** Two buttons.

Sewing: If desired, prepare pockets and topstitch them in place. Overlock outer edge of each facing, stitch them under arms, clip the seam allowance at corners almost to the stitching line, turn right side out and press, topstitch facings in place. Stitch center front and center back seams. Stitch pleated upper edge to frontband and straps (see #7). Stitch inner leg seams. Make buttonholes and sew on buttons. Overlock leg ends, press them under and topstitch in place. (For a little girl, consider adding pretty ruffles to pocket edges and shoulder straps, especially if you are using calico, eyelet or seersucker for this pattern.)

17. SUMMER DRESS (or skirt)
Size: 4

Shirred upper edge, ruffle around lower edge, narrow tie-on straps, lace trim. (When too short, remove straps and use as a skirt with shirred upper edge becoming waist edge. Or, by using the same pattern, make a skirt with elasticized waist casing.)

Suggested fabrics: Lightweight crisp cotton types, batiste, seersucker, eyelet, calico, broadcloth, cotton knits. **Fabric required:** 60x90cm (2/3ydx36"). **Notions:** Elastic thread for shirring, lace. (Elastic for skirt waist.)

Sewing: Narrowly hem upper edge (unless cut on selvage), or bind the raw edge with folded lace. Stitch several rows of elastic shirring across upper edge (see page 33 for elastic shirring). Stitch center back seam. Overlock lower edge of ruffle and topstitch it under (or bind the raw edge with folded lace), stitch ends together into a circle, gather upper edge and stitch it to lower edge of dress. Prepare shoulder straps and stitch them in place under upper edge of front and back. Or use lace as shoulder straps and, if it is too narrow, zigzag two lengths of lace together side-by-side.

Need piping trim? Try encasing cord or yarn by sewing bias tape around it.

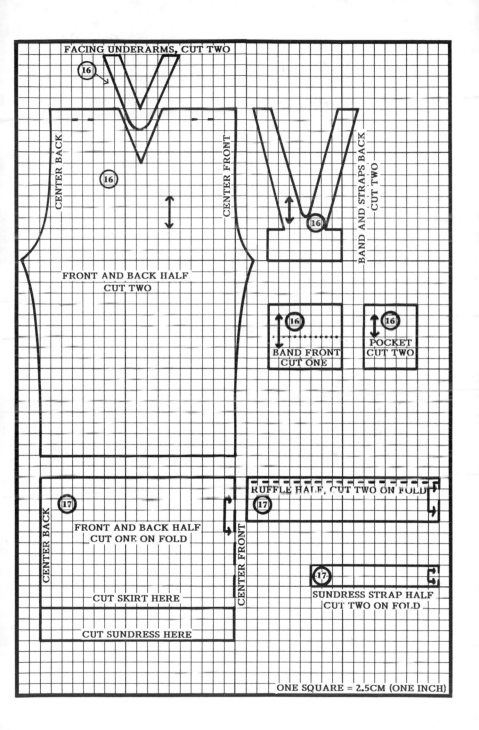

FACING UNDERARMS, CUT TWO

⑯

CENTER BACK

⑯

CENTER FRONT

BAND AND STRAPS BACK CUT TWO

⑯

FRONT AND BACK HALF
CUT TWO

⑯ BAND FRONT
CUT ONE

⑯ POCKET
CUT TWO

CENTER BACK

⑰

FRONT AND BACK HALF
CUT ONE ON FOLD

CENTER FRONT

CUT SKIRT HERE

CUT SUNDRESS HERE

RUFFLE HALF, CUT TWO ON FOLD

⑰

⑰ SUNDRESS STRAP HALF
CUT TWO ON FOLD

ONE SQUARE = 2.5CM (ONE INCH)

73

18. APRON/SUNDRESS/JUMPER
Size: 4

Wrap-around style, back sections overlap. Pull the left tie from back through buttonhole and tie at front.
Suggested fabrics: Cotton, eyelet, seersucker, calico, broadcloth, pinwale corduroy, soft denim, lightweight quilted fabrics (also fabric backed vinyl for craft apron).
Fabric required: 60x90cm (2/3ydx36"). **Notions:** Doublefold bias tape.

Sewing: Bind underarms and bib edges with bias tape. Overlock lower edge and sides, press them under and stitch in place. Make only one buttonhole (in the right side as shown on the pattern). Fold neck strap in half lengthwise right side in, stitch sides together, turn right side out and press, stitch each end securely under bib corners (the strap seam points toward the neck). Prepare ties and stitch them in place at each side, slipstitch tie ends closed. Add an appliqué or pocket onto front if desired. If you use vinyl or quilted fabrics, also bind lower edge and sides with bias tape. If you use eyelet or other lightweight fabric, consider binding all raw edges with folded lace or trimming them with gathered eyelet ribbon.

Raw edges are easy to bind with lace ribbon if you choose lace with such a design that you can fold it in half lengthwise. Stitch it around fabric edge like bias tape.

19. NIGHTGOWN (or T-shirt, dress)
Size: 4

Front and back gathered into rib knit yoke. Straight neck edge. Short or long puffed sleeves with rib knit bands.
Suggested fabrics: Garment and sleeves can be made from both stretch and non-stretch fabrics: Cotton knits, fleece, cotton types, flannelette, seersucker. (Also stretch terry, velour, pinwale corduroy or eyelet for top or dress.) Yoke and sleevebands from stretch fabrics only: Rib knit or very stretchy cotton knit or stretch terry. (Flame-retardant fabrics are required by law on children's sleepwear.) **Fabric required:** 120x115cm (1 1/3 yd x 45"). **Notions:** Rib knit for yoke and sleevebands.

Sewing: Right sides together, stitch shoulder seams of yoke for 5cm (2") in from outside edges toward neck as shown in the pattern, lock the stitch securely at neck edge. Fold yokes right side out, each one in half, so you have the neck opening in the middle. Gather front and back upper edges and stitch them to yoke. Gather sleeve tops and stitch them to armholes. Stitch sides and underarms. Stitch rib knit bands to sleeve ends. Overlock lower edge, press it under and topstitch in place.

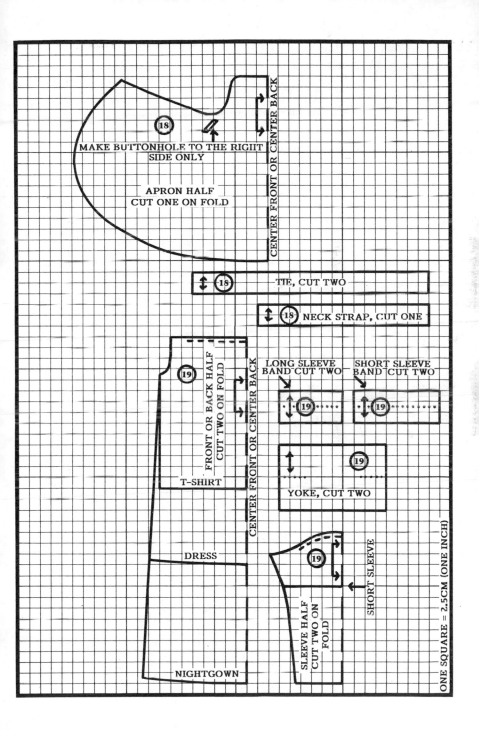

MAKE BUTTONHOLE TO THE RIGHT
SIDE ONLY

APRON HALF
CUT ONE ON FOLD

CENTER FRONT OR CENTER BACK

TIE, CUT TWO

NECK STRAP, CUT ONE

FRONT OR BACK HALF
CUT TWO ON FOLD

CENTER FRONT OR CENTER BACK

T-SHIRT

DRESS

NIGHTGOWN

LONG SLEEVE
BAND CUT TWO

SHORT SLEEVE
BAND CUT TWO

YOKE, CUT TWO

SHORT SLEEVE

SLEEVE HALF
CUT TWO ON
FOLD

ONE SQUARE = 2.5CM (ONE INCH)

20. BLOUSE
Size: 4

Long raglan sleeves. Elasticized eyelet trim around neck and sleeve ends forming self ruffles.
Suggested fabrics: Indian cotton, eyelet, batiste, crepe, seersucker, lightweight cotton types, cotton knits. **Fabric required:** 1mx90cm (1ydx36"). **Notions:** 165x5cm (65x2") eyelet trim (with openings for ribbon), 100cm (40") long piece of narrow satin ribbon, narrow elastic.

Sewing: Overlock sleeve ends and stitch eyelet trim to them. On inside, stitch a 15cm (6") long piece of stretched elastic to seam allowances of each sleeve end (between fabric and eyelet), forming self ruffles. Stitch sleeves to armhole edges of front and back. Stitch sides and underarms. Overlock neck opening and stitch eyelet trim around it. On inside, stitch stretched elastic to the seam allowance around neck (between fabric and eyelet) forming self ruffle. Overlock lower edge of blouse, press it under and topstitch in place. Insert satin ribbon through eyelet trim around neck, tie it in front.

21. DRESS
Size: 4

Short or long raglan sleeves. Rib knit bands around neck, sleeve ends and between raglan seams. Rib knit waistband between bodice and gathered skirt.
Stretch fabrics only: Stretch terry, velour, cotton knits. Also fleece. **Fabric required:** 1mx115cm (1ydx45"). **Notions:** Rib knit.

Sewing: Stitch rib knit bands between raglan sleeves and armhole edges of front and back. Stitch sides and underarms. Stitch rib knit bands around sleeve ends and neck. Stitch waistband into a circle, and try it on the child; take in if necessary (it should fit snugly). Stitch upper edge of waistband to bodice. Stitch skirt side seams, stitch the skirt to lower edge of waistband, stretching waistband to divide fullness evenly. Overlock lower edge of dress, press it under and topstitch in place.

22. T-SHIRT
Size: 4

Straight top with short or long sleeves, rib knit bands around short sleeve ends and neck.
Stretch fabrics only: Cotton knits, stretch terry, velour. (Enlarge the pattern for non-stretch mesh fabrics.) **Fabric required:** 50x140cm (½ydx55"). **Notions:** Rib knit.

Sewing: If desired, sew an appliqué onto front or sleeves. Stitch shoulder seams. Stitch sleeves to armholes. Stitch sides and underarms. Stitch rib knit bands around short sleeve ends and neck. Overlock lower edge (and long sleeve ends), press under and topstitch in place.

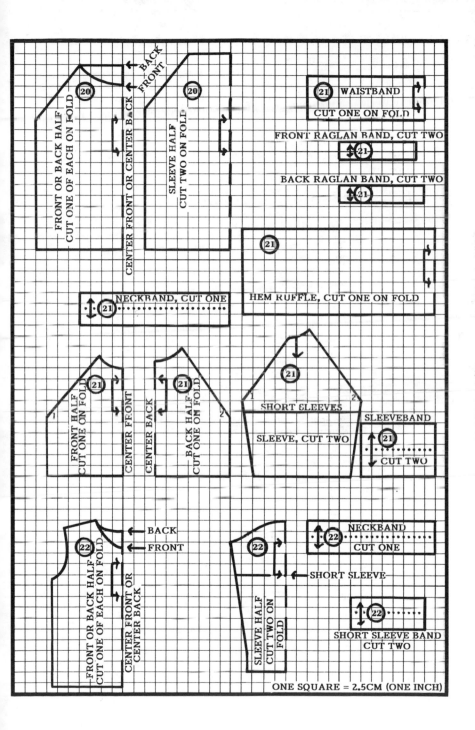

BACK
FRONT

20 FRONT OR BACK HALF CUT ONE OF EACH ON FOLD

CENTER FRONT OR CENTER BACK

20 SLEEVE HALF CUT TWO ON FOLD

21 WAISTBAND
CUT ONE ON FOLD

FRONT RAGLAN BAND, CUT TWO
21

BACK RAGLAN BAND, CUT TWO
21

21

HEM RUFFLE, CUT ONE ON FOLD

21 NECKBAND, CUT ONE • • • • • • • • • • • • • • •

21 FRONT HALF CUT ONE ON FOLD

CENTER FRONT

CENTER BACK

21 BACK HALF CUT ONE ON FOLD

21 SHORT SLEEVES
SLEEVE, CUT TWO

SLEEVEBAND
21 • • • • • • • •
CUT TWO

BACK
FRONT

22 FRONT OR BACK HALF CUT ONE OF EACH ON FOLD

CENTER FRONT OR CENTER BACK

22

SLEEVE HALF CUT TWO ON FOLD

SHORT SLEEVE

22 NECKBAND • • • • • • • • • • • • • • •
CUT ONE

22 • • • • • •
SHORT SLEEVE BAND
CUT TWO

ONE SQUARE = 2.5CM (ONE INCH)

77

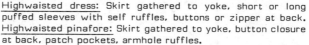

23. DRESS AND PINAFORE
Size: 4

Highwaisted dress: Skirt gathered to yoke, short or long puffed sleeves with self ruffles, buttons or zipper at back.
Highwaisted pinafore: Skirt gathered to yoke, button closure at back, patch pockets, armhole ruffles.
Suggested fabrics: Dress - Cotton types, eyelet, pinwale corduroy, batiste, lace, seersucker, velour, cotton knits. Pinafore - Cotton types, eyelet, lace, batiste, seersucker.
Fabric required: Dress with long sleeves - 120x115cm (1 1/4 ydx45"). Pinafore - 1mx115cm (1ydx45"). **Notions:** Dress - Three buttons or 20cm (8") long zipper, elastic, doublefold bias tape. (Lace for neck opening.) Pinafore - Buttons, doublefold bias tape.

Sewing: Hem sleeve ends narrowly. On inside, stitch stretched elastic about 5cm (2") from sleeve ends, forming self ruffles. Stitch shoulder seams. Gather sleeve tops and stitch them to armholes. Stitch sides and underarms. Stitch skirt side seams. Gather upper edge of skirt and stitch it to yoke. Stitch skirt center back seam, leaving 8cm (3") open at upper end of seam. Add buttons and buttonholes, or zipper, at opening. Overlock lower edge of dress, press it under and topstitch in place. Depending on fabric, finish the neck edge with bias tape or folded lace or facing. Or sew Peter Pan collar (pattern shown) from self fabric (or contrasting fabric) and stitch it around neck with bias tape.
Sewing pinafore: Prepare pockets and topstitch them in place. Stitch shoulder seams. Gather curved edges of armhole ruffles and stitch them to armholes, trim seam with bias tape. Stitch side seams of yoke. Stitch side seams of skirt. Gather skirt upper edge and stitch it to yoke. Finish raw neck edge with bias tape. Overlock center back edges and lower edge, topstitch them under. Add buttons and buttonholes at back.

24. SUN BONNET
Size: 4

Large, puffed headpiece gathered to brim, elasticized back, tie-on ribbons.
Suggested fabrics: Lightweight cotton types, batiste, seersucker, eyelet, calico. **Fabric required:** 50x115cm (½ydx45"). **Notions:** Elastic, fusible interfacing, two 25cm (10") long ribbons (or make them from self fabric).

Sewing: Iron interfacing to wrong side of one brim. Stitch brims together, trim curves, turn right side out and press. (Topstitch entire brim with multiple rows if desired.) Zigzag stretched elastic along straight neck edge, turn it under and stitch in place. Gather round edge of headpiece and stitch it to brim. Sew ribbons in place.

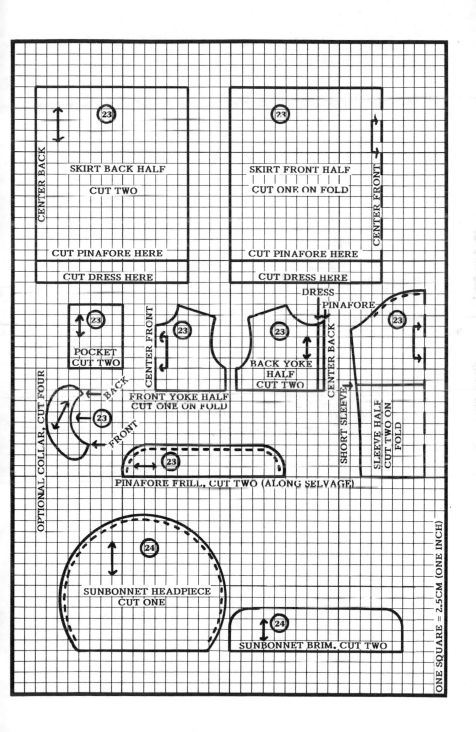

SKIRT BACK HALF
CUT TWO

CENTER BACK

CUT PINAFORE HERE
CUT DRESS HERE

SKIRT FRONT HALF
CUT ONE ON FOLD

CENTER FRONT

CUT PINAFORE HERE
CUT DRESS HERE

DRESS
PINAFORE

POCKET
CUT TWO

CENTER FRONT

FRONT YOKE HALF
CUT ONE ON FOLD

BACK YOKE
HALF
CUT TWO

CENTER BACK

OPTIONAL COLLAR, CUT FOUR

BACK

FRONT

SHORT SLEEVE

SLEEVE HALF
CUT TWO ON
FOLD

PINAFORE FRILL, CUT TWO (ALONG SELVAGE)

SUNBONNET HEADPIECE
CUT ONE

SUNBONNET BRIM, CUT TWO

ONE SQUARE = 2.5CM (ONE INCH)

25. PULL-ON PANTS AND SHORTS (or pajama pants)
Size: 4

Straight legs, no side seams, elasticized waist casing, rib knit legbands. (If pants are long enough without rib knit bands, sew casings in leg ends for elastic and lengthen pants later with rib knit bands. When too short, make them into shorts.)

Stretch fabrics only: Stretch terry, velour, cotton knits. Also fleece. **Fabric required:** Pants - 70x90cm (3/4 ydx36"); shorts - 35x90cm (14x36"). **Notions:** Wide elastic for waist, rib knit for legbands. (Optional decorative tape for sides.)

Sewing: If desired, stitch colorful decorative tape down sides. Stitch center front and center back seams. Stitch inner leg seams. Sew waist edge down to form casing and insert elastic. Pants: Stitch rib knit bands to leg ends. Shorts: Overlock leg ends, press them under and topstitch in place.

26. SWEATSHIRT (or pajama top)
Size: 4

Loose-fitting straight top with long raglan sleeves, rib knit bands around sleeve ends, neck and waist. (Optional: Add drawstring hood and kangaroo pocket.)

Stretch fabrics only: Stretch terry, velour, cotton knits. Also fleece. **Fabric required:** 50x140cm (½ydx55"). **Notions:** Rib knit, optional decorative tape.

Sewing: If desired, sew an appliqué onto front or sleeves, or stitch decorative tape across chest. Stitch sleeves to armhole edges of front and back. Stitch sides and underarms. Stitch rib knit bands into circles, fold in half lengthwise right side out, and stitch them around sleeve ends, neck and waist.

To avoid puckers, never glide the iron when applying fusible interfacing.

Affix an appliqué or a patch securely in place with a strip of fusible web so you can stitch around it without pins.

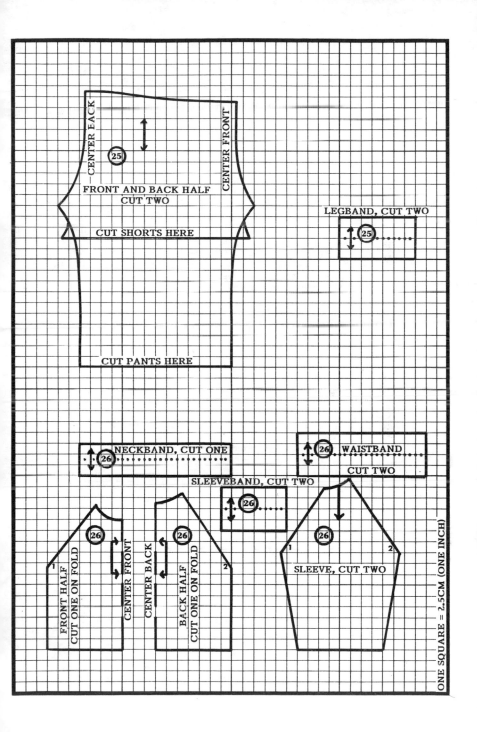

CENTER BACK

㉕

CENTER FRONT

FRONT AND BACK HALF
CUT TWO

CUT SHORTS HERE

LEGBAND, CUT TWO

㉕

CUT PANTS HERE

㉖ NECKBAND, CUT ONE

㉖ WAISTBAND

CUT TWO

SLEEVEBAND, CUT TWO

㉖

㉖

㉖

FRONT HALF
CUT ONE ON FOLD

CENTER FRONT

CENTER BACK

BACK HALF
CUT ONE ON FOLD

1

2

㉖

SLEEVE, CUT TWO

1

2

ONE SQUARE = 2.5CM (ONE INCH)

81

27. OVERALLS
Size: 4

Straight legs, no side seams, zippered front, kangaroo pockets, buttoned straps. (Lengthen with rib knit bands.)
Suggested fabrics: Mediumweight cotton types, corduroy, denim, quilted fabrics, fleece, windproof and water repellent fabrics. **Fabric required:** 120x115m (1 1/4 ydx45"). **Notions:** 25cm (10") long zipper, two buttons.

Sewing: Overlock pocket bias edges, press and stitch them under, press remaining raw edges under, topstitch pockets in place. Stitch zipper in place. Stitch center front seam below zipper. Stitch center back seam. Stitch inner leg seams. Sew straps ready. Pin facing in place, straps in between (so that they slant toward shoulders from back), stitch through all thicknesses. Turn right side out, press facing to inside, topstitch entire upper edge. Stitch facing ends under along each side of the zipper. Catch facing in place under arms with vertical topstitching. Add buttons and buttonholes. Overlock leg ends, press them under and topstitch in place.

28. JACKET (or coat, vest, bathrobe) AND BALACLAVA HELMET
Size: 4

Kangaroo pockets, drawstring hood, zippered front, rib knit cuffs. Optional elasticized waist. (Lengthen the pattern for coat and bathrobe. Vest: Omit sleeves and hood; add rib knit bands to armholes, neck edge, and shortened hem; add snap fasteners to front.) Balaclava helmet has rib knit band around face opening.
Suggested fabrics: Jacket - Fleece, mediumweight cotton types, denim, nylon, corduroy, quilted fabrics, windproof and water repellent fabrics. (Bathrobe: Terry, stretch terry, velour, fleece.) Stretch fabrics only for balaclava helmet: Stretch terry, velour, cotton knits, acrylic knits, rib knit. **Fabric required:** Jacket - 1mx115cm (1ydx45"). Balaclava helmet - 50x90cm (½ydx36"). **Notions:** Jacket - Rib knit, 40cm (16") long separating zipper, 2 metres (2 1/4 yards) of cord. Balaclava helmet - Rib knit for band.

Sewing jacket: Overlock pocket bias edges, stitch them under, press upper edges and short sides under, and topstitch pockets in place. (Bind quilted fabric edges with bias tape.) Stitch shoulder seams. Stitch sleeves to armholes. Stitch sides and underarms. Stitch hood center seam, stitch hood to neck edge. Press under front edges of jacket and hood's lower front edges; stitch zipper in place. Overlock lower edge, stitch it under forming a casing. Stitch rib knit bands to sleeve ends. Stitch rib knit band around face opening, forming a casing. Cut the cord in two, insert through hood and hem casings.
Sewing balaclava helmet: Stitch center front and center back seams. Overlock lower edge. Stitch rib knit band around face opening.

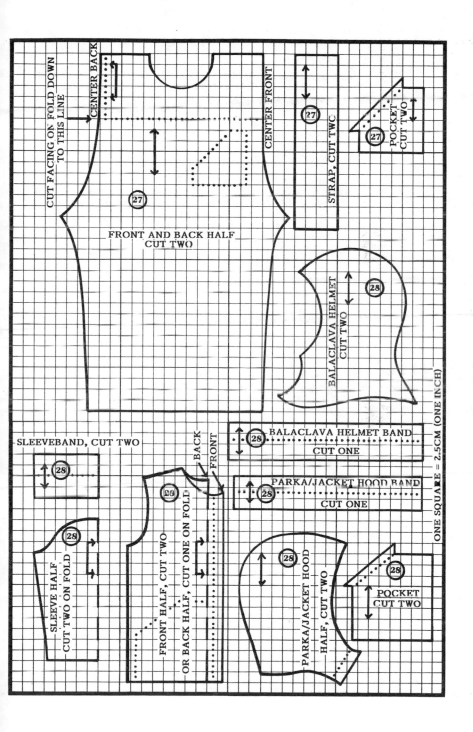

CUT FACING ON FOLD DOWN
TO THIS LINE

CENTER BACK

CENTER FRONT

27

FRONT AND BACK HALF
CUT TWO

27

STRAP, CUT TWO

27

POCKET
CUT TWO

27

BALACLAVA HELMET
CUT TWO

28

SLEEVEBAND, CUT TWO

28

BACK

FRONT

BALACLAVA HELMET BAND
CUT ONE

28

PARKA/JACKET HOOD BAND
CUT ONE

28

28

FRONT HALF, CUT TWO

OR BACK HALF, CUT ONE ON FOLD

28

SLEEVE HALF
CUT TWO ON FOLD

28

PARKA/JACKET HOOD
HALF, CUT TWO

28

POCKET
CUT TWO

28

ONE SQUARE = 2.5CM (ONE INCH)

83

29. MAILLOT/BODYSUIT
Size: 4

Simple design. Easy pattern to cut apart vertically, horizontally or on the bias when you wish to use more than one color (just remember to add seam allowances to all newly-made seams prior to cutting out the fabric). Add pretty ruffle if desired.
Two-way stretch knits only: Spandex. (Cut crosswise if the maximum stretch is in fabric's length.) **Fabric required:** 50x50cm (20x20"). **Notions:** Narrow swimsuit elastic.

Sewing: Sew an appliqué onto front if desired. Stitch crotch seam. Stitch side seams and shoulders. On inside, zigzag slightly stretched elastic around legholes, armholes and neck opening. Turn elasticized edges under and edgestitch in place. (If you wish to trim edges with a different color, stitch elastic as explained above and bind elasticized edges with bifold stretch tape; see page 35. Prior to sewing the seams, add extra crotch piece if desired, as for swimtrunks #30.)

30. SWIMTRUNKS
Size: 4

Simple design, crotch reinforced, facings around legholes, elasticized waist casing. Easy pattern to cut apart vertically, horizontally or on the bias, if you wish to use more than one color (just remember to add seam allowances to all newly-made seams prior to cutting out the fabric).
Two-way stretch knits only: Spandex. (Cut crosswise if the maximum stretch is in fabric's length.) **Fabric required:** 50x50cm (20x20"). **Notions:** Wide swimsuit elastic for waist.

Sewing: Sew an appliqué onto front if desired. Reinforce crotch by stitching extra crotch piece to the wrong side of the garment. Overlock outer edge of each facing, stitch the facings around legholes. Stitch sides and facing ends. Turn facings to inside and topstitch them in place around legholes. Sew waist edge into a casing and insert elastic.

> When you stop your sewing machine to rearrange the fabric, leave the needle down so the stitching line doesn't shift.

> Before you cut out expensive fabric or an unusual pattern, test it first in inexpensive fabric.

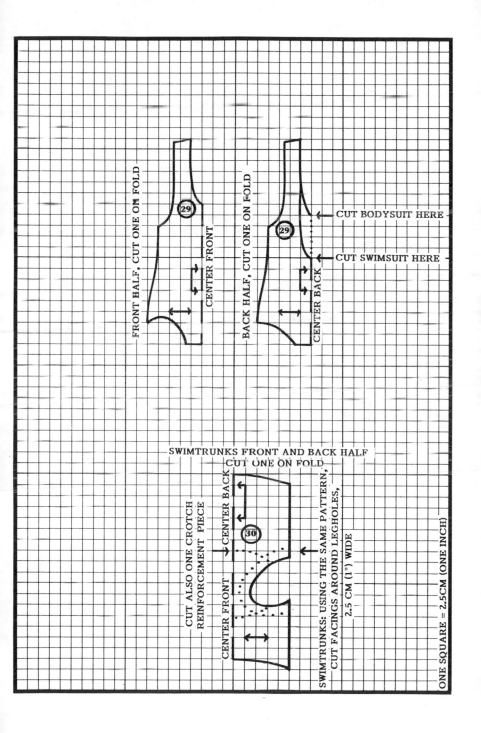

FRONT HALF, CUT ONE ON FOLD

CENTER FRONT

BACK HALF, CUT ONE ON FOLD

CENTER BACK

29

29

CUT BODYSUIT HERE

CUT SWIMSUIT HERE

SWIMTRUNKS FRONT AND BACK HALF
CUT ONE ON FOLD

CENTER BACK

CUT ALSO ONE CROTCH
REINFORCEMENT PIECE

CENTER FRONT

30

SWIMTRUNKS: USING THE SAME PATTERN,
CUT FACINGS AROUND LEGHOLES,
2.5 CM (1") WIDE

ONE SQUARE = 2.5CM (ONE INCH)

31. WRAP-AROUND SKIRT
Size: 6

Back sections overlap, waistband continues into ties for front tying.

Suggested fabrics: Cotton types, calico, broadcloth, pinwale corduroy, denim, velour, cotton knits, fleece. **Fabric required:** 1mx115cm (40x45").

Sewing: Stitch side seams. Overlock lower edge and back edges, press them under narrowly and topstitch in place. Stitch center front seam of waistband. Pin waistband to skirt (right side of band against wrong side of skirt, center fronts matching, raw edges even, ties extending at each side), stitch. Fold each tie in half lengthwise right side in, stitch ends and sides closed, turn right side out, press. Press waistband seam allowance under and topstitch it closed. Sew one slanted buttonhole in waistband (shown in the pattern).

32. PEASANT BLOUSE
(or dress, nightgown)
Size: 6

Puffed short sleeves. Elasticized neck opening and sleeve ends forming self ruffles. Lace trim. If desired, decorate the garment with machine embroidery, appliqués or fabric paints, or trim it with colorful ribbons. (Lengthen the pattern for dress or nightie. Stitch stretched elastic around hips for the dress, and add long satin ribbon.)

Suggested fabrics: Indian cotton, cotton types, calico, broadcloth, batiste, eyelet, cotton knits. (Also flannelette for nightgown.) **Fabric required:** 70x115cm (3/4ydx45"). **Notions:** Lace, narrow elastic.

Sewing: Stitch shoulder seams. Gather sleeve tops and stitch them to armholes. Trim sleeve ends and neck opening with lace. On inside, stitch stretched elastic to sleeve ends and neck opening, 2.5cm (1") from edges, forming self ruffles. (The elastic length for sleeve ends: 18cm or 7"; neck opening: 43cm or 17".) Stitch sides and underarms. Hem lower edge narrowly.

33. CAMISOLE
(or dress, nightgown)
Size: 6

Lace trim, narrow shoulder straps. (Lengthen the pattern for nightie. Add two or three rows of gathered tiers around lower edge for a minidress.)

Stretch fabrics only: Cotton knits, stretch terry, velour, rib knit. **Fabric required:** 50x90cm (½ydx36"). **Notions:** Lace.

Sewing: Trim upper edge with lace. Stitch center back seam. Hem lower edge narrowly. Make shoulder straps from fabric or lace and stitch them in place.

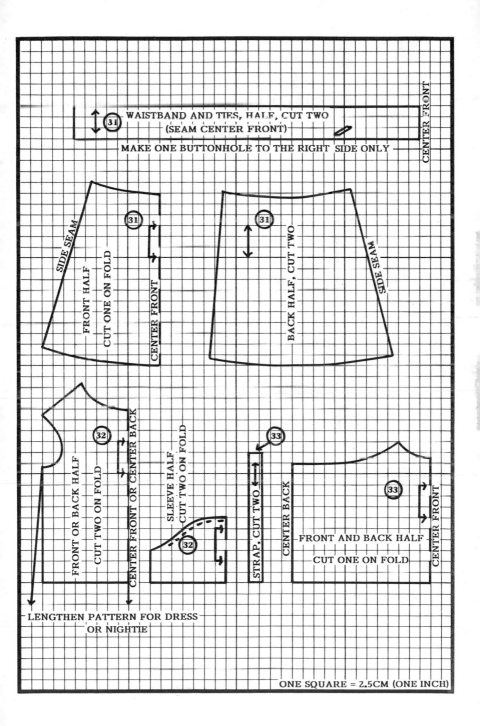

WAISTBAND AND TIES, HALF, CUT TWO
(SEAM CENTER FRONT)
MAKE ONE BUTTONHOLE TO THE RIGHT SIDE ONLY

CENTER FRONT

FRONT HALF
CUT ONE ON FOLD
SIDE SEAM
CENTER FRONT

BACK HALF, CUT TWO
SIDE SEAM

FRONT OR BACK HALF
CUT TWO ON FOLD
CENTER FRONT OR CENTER BACK

SLEEVE HALF
CUT TWO ON FOLD

STRAP, CUT TWO

CENTER BACK
FRONT AND BACK HALF
CUT ONE ON FOLD
CENTER FRONT

LENGTHEN PATTERN FOR DRESS
OR NIGHTIE

ONE SQUARE = 2.5CM (ONE INCH)

87

34. SUMMER DRESS
Size: 6

Three rows of tiers gathered to crosswise upper bodice band, lace trim, narrow shoulder straps.
Suggested fabrics: Lightweight cotton types, calico, broadcloth, batiste, seersucker, eyelet, cotton knits. **Fabric required:** 120x115cm [1 1/3 ydx45"]. **Notions:** Lace.

Sewing: Stitch band center back seam, press the band in half wrong sides together and raw edges even. Stitch each tier into a circle. Gather and stitch upper tier to band. Gather and stitch middle tier to upper tier. Gather and stitch lower tier to middle tier. Trim lower edge with lace. Sew straps from self fabric, lace or ribbon and stitch them in place.

35. SUMMER DRESS
Size: 6

V-neck, tie-gathers at shoulders, rounded hemline slits, elasticized waist. [Cut shorter for top, lengthen for nightie.]
Suggested fabrics: Cotton types, calico, broadcloth, seersucker, pinwale corduroy, cotton knits. **Fabric required:** 1mx115cm [1ydx45"]. **Notions:** Elastic for waist.

Sewing: Overlock armhole edges, all four separately, press under 1.3cm [½"] and topstitch in place. Stitch shoulder seams with 2cm [3/4"] seam allowances, press seams open and stitch, forming two casings on each shoulder. Prepare ties, cut each in two. Insert ties through shoulder casings, attach ends to casing ends at neck. Stitch neck facing into a circle, overlock outer edge, stitch facing to neck edge, press to inside and topstitch in place. Stitch side seams. Overlock lower edge and side slits, stitch them under narrowly. On inside, stitch stretched elastic around waist.

36. KNICKERALLS
Size: 6

Knee-length jumpsuit. Elasticized waist, upper edge and knees. Shoulder ties.
Suggested fabrics: Cotton types, calico, broadcloth, eyelet, seersucker, cotton knits, velour, fleece. **Fabric required:** 1mx115cm [1ydx45"]. **Notions:** Narrow elastic.

Sewing: Stitch center front and center back seams. Stitch inner leg seams. Sew casings in leg ends and upper edge and insert elastic. On inside, stitch stretched elastic around waist. Sew straps ready and stitch them in place to tie over shoulders.

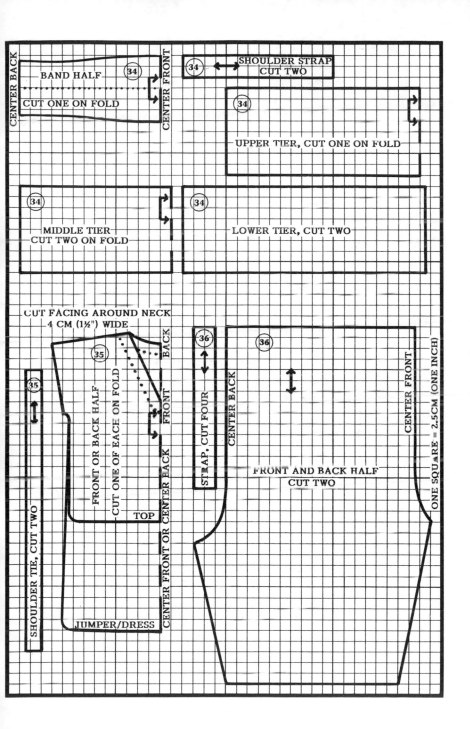

CENTER BACK

BAND HALF

CUT ONE ON FOLD

CENTER FRONT

(34)

(34) SHOULDER STRAP
CUT TWO

(34)

UPPER TIER, CUT ONE ON FOLD

(34)

MIDDLE TIER
CUT TWO ON FOLD

(34)

LOWER TIER, CUT TWO

CUT FACING AROUND NECK
4 CM (1½") WIDE

(35)

BACK

FRONT OR BACK HALF

CUT ONE OF EACE ON FOLD

FRONT

TOP

CENTER FRONT OR CENTER BACK

(35)

SHOULDER TIE, CUT TWO

JUMPER/DRESS

(36)

STRAP, CUT FOUR

CENTER BACK

(36)

FRONT AND BACK HALF
CUT TWO

CENTER FRONT

ONE SQUARE = 2.5CM (ONE INCH)

37. NIGHTGOWN
(or blouse, dress)
Size: 6

Loose-fitting nightgown, long raglan sleeves with self-ruffled sleeve ends, elasticized self-ruffled neck opening. (Lace-trimmed blouse. Dress has rib knit bands around neck opening and sleeve ends.)
Suggested fabrics: Lightweight cotton types, flannelette, seersucker, batiste, eyelet, cotton knits, Indian cotton. (Also fleece, velour, pinwale corduroy for dress.) **Fabric required:** Long nightie with long sleeves - 140x115cm (1½ydx45"). **Notions:** Narrow elastic. (Rib knit for dress. Lace for blouse.)

Sewing: Stitch sleeves to armhole edges of front and back. Stitch sides and underarms. Narrowly hem sleeve ends and neck edge, or bind them with folded lace. On inside, stitch stretched elastic to sleeve ends and neck opening (2.5cm or 1" from the edge), forming self ruffles. Overlock lower edge, press it under and topstitch in place.

38. HOODED BATHROBE
(or coat, jacket)
Size: 6

Short or long raglan sleeves, patch pockets, hood, optional buttons and belt.
Suggested fabrics: Terry, stretch terry, velour, fleece, quilted fabrics. (Corduroy, denim, mediumweight cotton types, nylon, wool duffle, windproof and water repellent fabrics for coat or jacket.) **Fabric required:** Long bathrobe with long sleeves - 2mx115cm (2ydx45"). **Notions:** Five buttons. (Jacket or coat: Buttons or snap fasteners or separating zipper.)

Sewing: Prepare pockets and topstitch them in place. Stitch sleeves to armhole edges of front and back. Stitch sides and underarms. Stitch hood center back seam. Stitch hood to neck opening. Overlock front edges and hood front edge. Press under and stitch in place 4cm (1½") from front edges of bathrobe and hood. Overlock sleeve ends and lower edge, press them under and topstitch in place. Add buttons and buttonholes. Or sew a belt. The belt will stay in place better if you sew a casing instead of carriers (finished casing width as wide as the belt) across the back stitched in place on the right side of fabric. (Jacket and coat: Add drawstring to hood casing - see design #6. Consider placing drawstring in lower edge of jacket also.)

> Easy shirring with no breakage: Zigzag wide stitches over, not through, cord (or buttonhole twist, strong nylon thread or dental floss). Attach one end securely, then gather the fabric by pulling the other end of the cord.

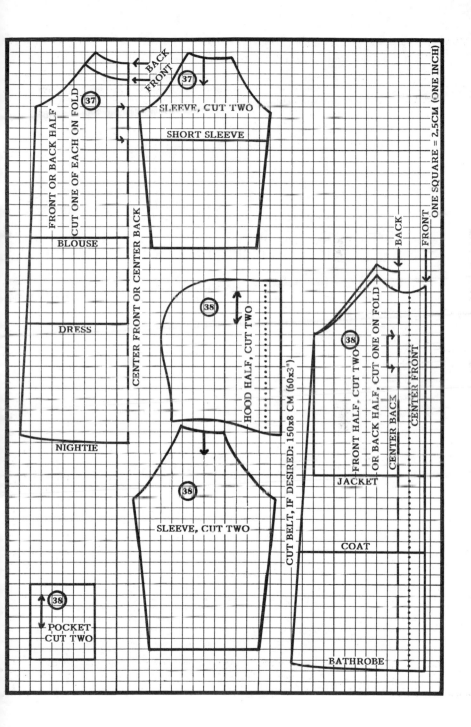

BACK
FRONT
SLEEVE, CUT TWO
SHORT SLEEVE

FRONT OR BACK HALF
CUT ONE OF EACH ON FOLD

BLOUSE

DRESS

CENTER FRONT OR CENTER BACK

NIGHTIE

HOOD HALF, CUT TWO

CUT BELT, IF DESIRED: 150x8 CM (60x3")

SLEEVE, CUT TWO

POCKET
CUT TWO

ONE SQUARE = 2.5CM (ONE INCH)

BACK
FRONT

FRONT HALF, CUT TWO
OR BACK HALF, CUT ONE ON FOLD

CENTER BACK

CENTER FRONT

JACKET

COAT

BATHROBE

91

39. SHORTS
Size: 6

Wide elasticized waist, rounded side slits.
Stretch fabrics only: Stretch terry, velour, cotton knits, rib knit. **Fabric required:** 50x90cm (½ydx36"). **Notions:** Wide elastic for waist. Contrasting doublefold bias (or stretch) tape 160cm (64").

Sewing: Stitch inner leg seams. Starting at lower side back edge, bind raw edges of lower leg and side front with bias tape (or bifold stretch tape made of contrasting stretch fabric; see page 35). On outside, lap front over back at side edges, topstitch to form side seams above rounded slits. Stitch center front and center back seams. Sew casing in waist edge and insert elastic.

40. T-SHIRT
(or dress, nightgown)
Size: 6

Entire upper edge of front and back bound with stretch tape. Straight bodice, boat neck, short sleeves. (Stitch short gathered skirt around lower edge for dress, or stitch rib knit between skirt and top. Lengthen the pattern for nightie.)
Stretch fabrics only: Cotton knits, acrylic knits, stretch terry, velour. **Fabric required:** 50x115cm (½ydx45").

Sewing: You'll need 105cm (42") of extra-wide bifold stretch tape made of self fabric (see page 35). Bind upper edges of both front and back (including shoulders) with the prepared bifold stretch tape. Lap front shoulder edges over back and topstitch them together. Stitch sleeves to armholes. Bind sleeve ends with bifold stretch tape. Stitch sides and underarms. Overlock lower edge, press it under and topstitch in place.

41. V-NECK TOP
(or dress, nightgown)
Size: 6

Neckband, short sleeves, patch pocket. (Lengthen pattern for dress or nightie. Elasticized waist for dress.)
Stretch fabrics only: Cotton knits, stretch terry, velour, acrylic knits. (Enlarge the pattern for non-stretch mesh fabrics.) **Fabric required:** 60x115cm (2/3ydx45").

Sewing: Sew an appliqué onto pocket, if desired. Sew pocket ready and topstitch it in place. Stitch sleeves to armhole edges of front and back. Stitch sides and underarms. Overlock sleeve ends and lower edge, press them under and topstitch in place. Turn the garment inside out. Stitch neckband into a circle, clip corner to stitching line. Press the band in half lengthwise right side out and stitch it around neck, stretching slightly to divide fabric fullness evenly.

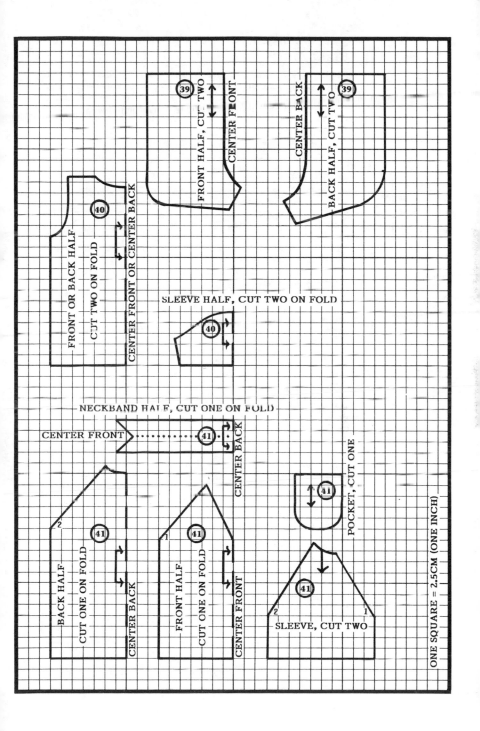

FRONT HALF, CUT TWO

CENTER FRONT

CENTER BACK

BACK HALF, CUT TWO

FRONT OR BACK HALF

CUT TWO ON FOLD

CENTER FRONT OR CENTER BACK

SLEEVE HALF, CUT TWO ON FOLD

NECKBAND HALF, CUT ONE ON FOLD

CENTER FRONT

CENTER BACK

POCKET, CUT ONE

BACK HALF

CUT ONE ON FOLD

CENTER BACK

FRONT HALF

CUT ONE ON FOLD

CENTER FRONT

SLEEVE, CUT TWO

ONE SQUARE = 2.5CM (ONE INCH)

93

42. JACKET (or coat)
Size: 6

Raglan sleeves, buttons or snap fasteners on front, kangaroo pockets. Rib knit bands around sleeve ends, neck and lower edge. (Lengthen the pattern for coat. Eliminate waistband and kangaroo pockets, and add regular patch pockets.)
Suggested fabrics: Corduroy, denim, quilted fabrics, fleece, mediumweight cotton types, nylon, windproof and water repellent fabrics. **Fabric required:** 1mx115cm (1ydx45"). **Notions:** Rib knit, buttons or snap fastener tape, interfacing.

Sewing: Iron interfacing to wrong sides of facing allowances at front edges. Overlock bias edge of each pocket, press and stitch them under; press under upper edges and long sides, and topstitch pockets in place. Stitch center slits closed at sleeve tops. Stitch sleeves to armhole edges of front and back. Stitch sides and underarms. Overlock front edges and press them under. Stitch rib knit bands to sleeve ends, lower edge and neck. Make buttonholes and sew on buttons (or snap fastener tape). If using quilted fabrics, trim pocket edges with bias tape or folded rib knit instead of pressing them under.

43. DRESS
Size: 6

Dropped waist, gathered skirt. Long or short gathered sleeves. Rib knit neckband and sleevebands.
Stretch fabrics only: Cotton knits, stretch terry, velour. Also fleece. **Fabric required:** 120x115cm (1 1/4 ydx45"). **Notions:** Rib knit.

Sewing: Stitch shoulder seams. Gather sleeve tops and stitch them to armholes. Stitch sides and underarms. Stitch skirt center back seam. Gather skirt upper edge and stitch it to the bodice. Stitch rib knit bands to sleeve ends and neck. Overlock lower edge, press it under and topstitch in place. (Variation: Cut bodice front and back double-layered and add soft fabric between the layers. Topstitch triple-layered bodice for a quilted trapunto-look prior to stitching the seams. Quilting the bodice will make it non-sretchy, so enlarge the neck opening slightly to be able to pull the dress on.)

Press trims and fabrics with raised design or nap from the wrong side over a soft terry towel to retain their three-dimensional appearance.

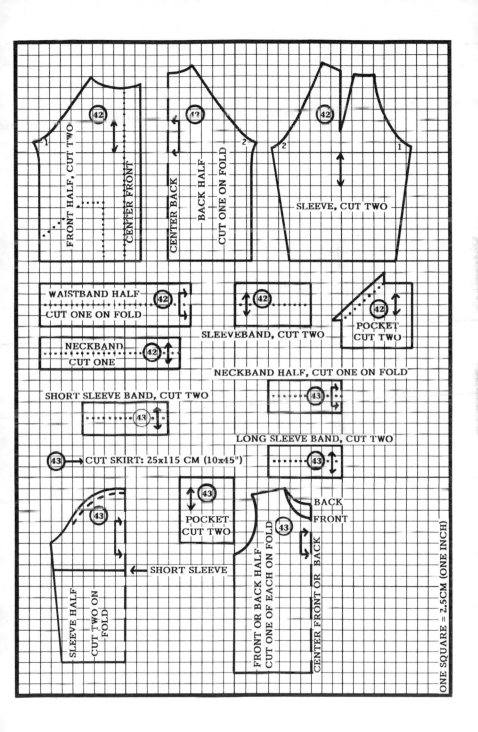

FRONT HALF, CUT TWO
CENTER FRONT
42

BACK HALF
CUT ONE ON FOLD
CENTER BACK
17

SLEEVE, CUT TWO
42

WAISTBAND HALF
CUT ONE ON FOLD
42

SLEEVEBAND, CUT TWO
42

POCKET
CUT TWO
42

NECKBAND
CUT ONE
42

NECKBAND HALF, CUT ONE ON FOLD

SHORT SLEEVE BAND, CUT TWO
43

LONG SLEEVE BAND, CUT TWO
43

CUT SKIRT: 25x115 CM (10x45")
43

POCKET
CUT TWO
43

BACK
FRONT
43

SHORT SLEEVE
43

SLEEVE HALF
CUT TWO ON FOLD

FRONT OR BACK HALF
CUT ONE OF EACH ON FOLD
CENTER FRONT OR BACK
43

ONE SQUARE = 2.5CM (ONE INCH)

95

44. SUSPENDER PANTS
Size: 6

Loose-fitting pants with straight legs, suspenders made of self fabric, patch pockets, elasticized waist with self-ruffled edge.
Suggested fabrics: Cotton types. **Fabric required:** 120x115cm (1 1/4 yd x 45"). **Notions:** Wide elastic, two buttons.

<u>Sewing:</u> Prepare pockets and topstitch them in place. Stitch side seams and inner leg seams. Stitch center front and center back seams. Narrowly hem waist edge. Measure a piece of elastic to fit snugly around child's waist, stitch ends together. Stitch the elastic around waist 2½cm (1") from hemmed waist edge (stitch close to both edges of elastic, stretching elastic while sewing). Hem the leg ends. Stitch long edges of suspenders, turn right side out and press. Stitch suspenders under waist front, make buttonholes in back ends and sew buttons on below waist back.

45. SUMMER DRESS
Size: 6

Simple sleeveless dress with self stretch binding around neck edge and armholes, ruffle around lower edge.
Stretch fabrics only: Cotton knits, stretch terry, velour.
Fabric required: Bodice – 60x115cm (2/3ydx45"); contrasting or same fabric for ruffle – 25x90cm (10x36").

<u>Sewing:</u> Stitch left shoulder seam. Bind neck opening with bifold stretch tape made of self fabric or contrasting fabric (see page 35). Stitch right shoulder seam. Bind armholes with bifold stretch tape. Stitch side seams. Sew ruffle ends together into a circle, overlock lower edge, press it under and topstitch in place; gather upper edge and stitch it around lower edge of bodice.

Tape a paper bag to sewing table's edge for quick scrap disposal.

When using stiff fabrics for ruffles, cut them on the bias or in a circular shape.

Recycle transparent milk bags to store patterns and notions.

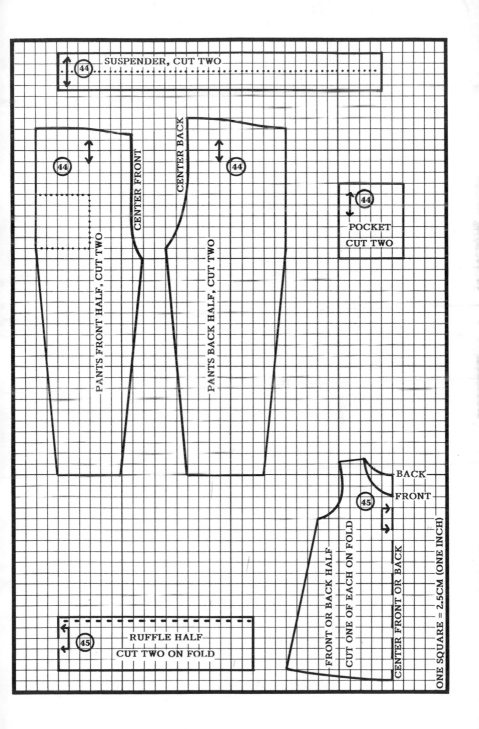

SUSPENDER, CUT TWO

44

44

CENTER FRONT

CENTER BACK

44

44
POCKET
CUT TWO

PANTS FRONT HALF, CUT TWO

PANTS BACK HALF, CUT TWO

BACK

FRONT

45

FRONT OR BACK HALF

CUT ONE OF EACH ON FOLD

CENTER FRONT OR BACK

ONE SQUARE = 2.5CM (ONE INCH)

45
RUFFLE HALF
CUT TWO ON FOLD

46. BIKINI
Size: 8

Top has gathered front with loop, string around neck continues through side casings and ties at back. Bottom has waistband forming elasticized casing, front ruffle and elasticized legholes.
Two-way stretch swimsuit fabric: Spandex. **Fabric required:** 60x90cm (2/3ydx36"). **Notions:** Narrow and wide swimsuit elastic.

Sewing top: Narrowly hem upper and lower edges. Stitch ends under forming side casings. Stitch loop side edges together, turn right side out and stitch ends together. Slip loop over bikini top to center front. Cut strips of fabric 2½cm (1") wide and sew them together for a string 125cm (50") long. Stitch long edges together, turn right side out. Insert the string through side casings (forming a loop behind the neck) and tie ends at back. Stitch string to casing lower ends so it stays in place.
(Sewing bottom: See next page.)

47. CAPE
Size: 8

Use absorbent fabrics to wear this cape over maillot. Or use warm soft fabrics to wear it with jeans.
Suggested fabrics: Terry, stretch terry, velour, knits, fleece, wool duffle. **Fabric required:** 140x90cm (55x36").
Notions: 5½m (6yd) of doublefold bias tape or foldover braid.

Sewing: Bind neck opening and all outer edges with bias tape or foldover braid. Fold cape in half at shoulders. On outside, topstitch under arms as shown.

48. SWIMTRUNKS
Size: 8

Simple basic pattern. (See also #30.)
Two-way stretch knits only: Spandex. **Fabric required:** 50x50cm (20x20"). **Notions:** Wide swimsuit elastic.

Sewing: On inside, stitch crotch piece in place. Overlock outer edge of each facing, stitch facings around legholes. Stitch side seams and facing ends. Turn facings to inside and topstitch them in place. Sew waist edge into a casing and insert elastic.

49. TANK TOP (or dress, nightie)
Size: 8

Simple sleeveless top, self stretch binding. (Lengthen for nightie. Add ruffled skirt to lower edge for a dress.)
Stretch fabrics only: Cotton knits, stretch terry, velour, rib knit. (Enlarge pattern slightly if you use non-stretch mesh fabric.) **Fabric required:** 60x90cm (2/3ydx36").

(Sewing tank top: See next page.)

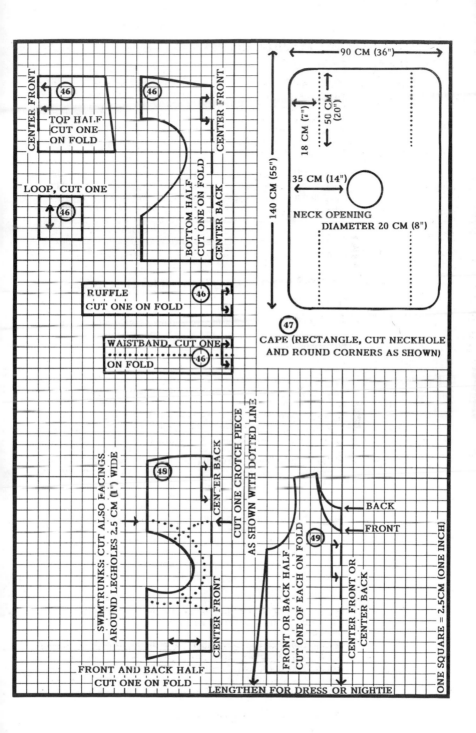

CENTER FRONT

(46)

TOP HALF
CUT ONE
ON FOLD

CENTER FRONT

(46)

LOOP, CUT ONE

(46)

BOTTOM HALF
CUT ONE ON FOLD

CENTER BACK

RUFFLE
CUT ONE ON FOLD

(46)

WAISTBAND, CUT ONE
ON FOLD

(46)

90 CM (36")

18 CM (7")

50 CM (20")

35 CM (14")

140 CM (55")

NECK OPENING
DIAMETER 20 CM (8")

(47)

CAPE (RECTANGLE, CUT NECKHOLE
AND ROUND CORNERS AS SHOWN)

SWIMTRUNKS: CUT ALSO FACINGS
AROUND LEGHOLES 2.5 CM (1") WIDE

(48)

CENTER BACK

CUT ONE CROTCH PIECE
AS SHOWN WITH DOTTED LINE

CENTER FRONT

FRONT AND BACK HALF
CUT ONE ON FOLD

BACK

FRONT

(49)

FRONT OR BACK HALF
CUT ONE OF EACH ON FOLD

CENTER FRONT OR
CENTER BACK

ONE SQUARE = 2.5CM (ONE INCH)

LENGTHEN FOR DRESS OR NIGHTIE

99

50. TOP (or dress)
Size: 8

Double-layered rib knit yoke, cap sleeves with bands. (Add single-layered rib knit waistband and ruffled skirt for a dress.)
Suggested fabrics: Cotton types. **Fabric required:** 60x115cm (2/3ydx45"). **Notions:** Rib knit.

Sewing: Stitch center front and center back seams. Stitch shoulder seams. Press all seam allowances to one side and topstitch in place. Stitch yoke layers together around neck edge, turn right side out and press. Stitch double-layered yoke to the garment. Press yoke seam allowances toward garment, topstitch in place. Stitch side seams. Stitch sleeveband ends together into a tube, press the bands in half wrong sides in and raw edges together. Turn the garment inside out and stitch the bands to sleeve ends. Hem lower edge narrowly.

51. PANTS OR BERMUDA SHORTS
Size: 8

Loose-fitting straight-legged pants or shorts have elasticized waist casing and in-seam pockets.
Suggested fabrics: Cotton types. **Fabric required:** 2mx90cm (2ydx36"). **Notions:** Wide elastic.

Sewing: Stitch pockets to front and back side edges. Stitch side seams and curved pocket edges. Press seam allowances and pockets toward front, baste pocket upper edges in place. Stitch inner leg seams. Stitch center front and center back seams. Overlock waist edge and leg ends. Press waist edge under along upper edges of pockets, stitch close to fold and along overlocked edge, forming a casing and insert elastic. Stitch vertically through all thicknesses at each seam (stitch-in-ditch) to prevent elastic from rolling. Hem leg ends.

Sewing bikini bottom (pattern #46 from previous page):
Hem lower edge of ruffle narrowly. Gather ruffle upper edge and stitch it to upper edge of pants front. Stitch side seams catching ruffle sides in between. Stitch gently stretched narrow elastic to legholes, turn elasticized edges under and edgestitch in place. Stitch waistband ends together, leaving an opening for elastic. Fold waistband in half right sides out and raw edges together, stitch it to waist edge (opening for elastic on wrong side). Insert elastic through waistband casing. Slipstitch opening closed.

Sewing tank top (pattern #49 from previous page):
Stitch left shoulder seam. Bind neck opening with bifold stretch tape made of self fabric (see page 35). Stitch right shoulder seam. Bind armholes with bifold stretch tape. Stitch side seams. Overlock lower edge, press it under and topstitch in place.

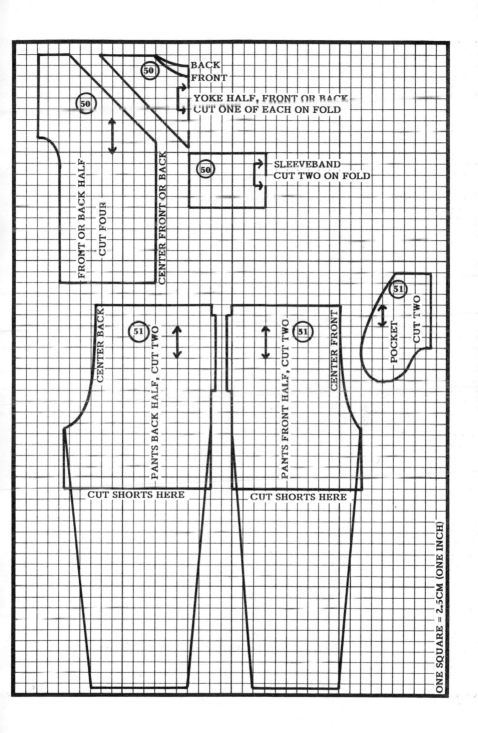

BACK
FRONT
YOKE HALF, FRONT OR BACK
CUT ONE OF EACH ON FOLD

SLEEVEBAND
CUT TWO ON FOLD

FRONT OR BACK HALF
CUT FOUR

CENTER FRONT OR BACK

CENTER BACK

PANTS BACK HALF, CUT TWO

PANTS FRONT HALF, CUT TWO

CENTER FRONT

POCKET
CUT TWO

CUT SHORTS HERE

CUT SHORTS HERE

ONE SQUARE = 2.5CM (ONE INCH)

50 50 50 51 51 51

101

52. VEST
Size: 8

Simple, one-piece pattern without side seams, with or
without lining. (Easy design to change: Cut front edges
straight and sew rib knit bands around neck, to front edges,
to armholes and to lower edge. Add buttons, buttonholes
and patch pockets. Decorate the vest with appliqués or
fabric paints, or trim it with ribbons.)
Suggested fabrics: Denim, corduroy, mediumweight cotton
types, quilted fabrics, synthetic leather or fur, velour,
fleece. **Fabric required:** 50x90cm (½ydx36"). Additional
fabric for lining (from any suitable, cotton-type fabric).
Notions: Doublefold bias tape.

Sewing: Unlined: With doublefold bias tape, bind all raw
edges of armholes, neck, front and lower edge. Stitch
shoulder seams. Lined: Stitch vest and lining together
around armholes and all edges, except shoulders, leaving
an opening at lower edge of center back. Trim corners
and clip curves, turn the garment right side out and press,
slipstitch opening closed. Stitch shoulder seams.

53. SHIRT
Size: 8

Loose-fitting shirt has short sleeves, yoke with extended
shoulders, easy notched collar, pocket. Suitable for both
boys and girls.
Suggested fabrics: Cotton types, seersucker, flannelette.
Fabric required: 1mx115cm (1ydx45"). **Notions:** Four buttons.

Sewing: Prepare pocket and topstitch it in place. Stitch
front and back sections to double-layered yoke. Stitch
sleeves to armholes. Stitch sides and underarms. Overlock
outer edges of front facing allowances. Press facings
to inside. Stitch collar layers together, trim corners, turn
right side out and press. Turn front facings to outside.
Pin collar to neck edge (center back of collar at center
back of neck edge) so that front edges of collar are
sandwiched between the garment and the front facing
allowances, stitch through all thicknesses, turn facings
to inside. Overlock lower edge and sleeve ends, press
them under narrowly and topstitch in place. Make
buttonholes and sew on buttons.

Trim mesh garment's hem with bias tape instead
of turning it under. For seams in mesh with very
big holes, sew narrow seams from right side of garment,
and cover them with doublefold bias tape.

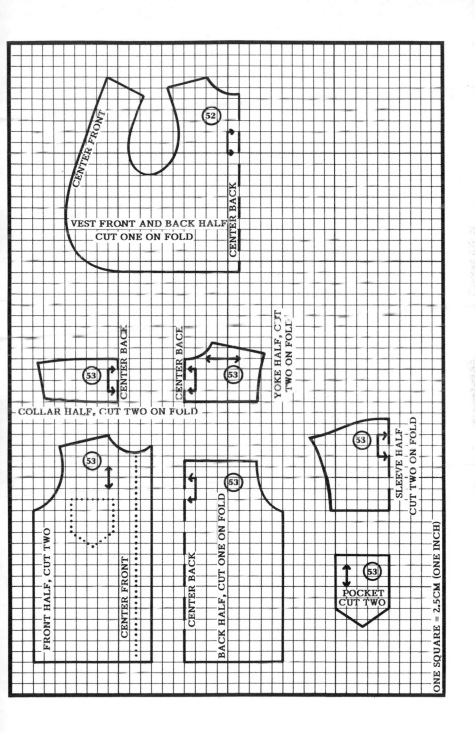

CENTER FRONT

52

CENTER BACK

VEST FRONT AND BACK HALF
CUT ONE ON FOLD

CENTER BACK

53

CENTER BACK

53

YOKE HALF, CUT
TWO ON FOLD

COLLAR HALF, CUT TWO ON FOLD

53

CENTER FRONT

FRONT HALF, CUT TWO

53

CENTER BACK

BACK HALF, CUT ONE ON FOLD

53

SLEEVE HALF
CUT TWO ON FOLD

53

POCKET
CUT TWO

ONE SQUARE = 2.5CM (ONE INCH)

54. PULL-ON PANTS OR SHORTS
(or pajama pants)
55. SWEATSHIRT OR PAJAMA TOP
Size: 8

Pants and shorts: Easy pattern without side seams, elastic at waist, rib knit bands around pantleg ends. Decorative trim at sides. (If pants are long enough without rib knit bands, sew elastic around ankles instead, and lengthen them next year with rib knit bands.) Sweatshirt: Short or long raglan sleeves. Rib knit bands around sleeve ends, neck and waist. Decorative trim.

Stretch fabrics only: Stretch terry, velour, acrylic knits, cotton knits. Also fleece. Fabric required: Pull-on pants and sweatshirt – 210x140cm (2 1/4 ydx55"); shorts 55x115cm (22x45"). Notions: Rib knit. Optional decorative trim.

Sewing pull-on pants: If desired, trim sides with contrasting tape. Stitch center back and center front seams. Stitch inner leg seams. Sew waist edge down into a casing and insert elastic. Stitch rib knit bands to leg ends. (Variation: Sew pockets to front before stitching the seams. Or sew a little pocket under waistline on inside for keys and money.)

Sewing shorts: Sew as pants except leg ends. Overlock leg ends, press them under and topstitch in place.

Sewing sweatshirt: If desired, trim front or sleeves with contrasting tape (or sew an appliqué or monogram onto front). Stitch sleeves to armhole edges of front and back. Stitch sides and underarms. Stitch rib knit bands around sleeve ends, neck and waist.

Permanently glue an extra measuring tape to the edge of your sewing table. Practical!

Cut tiny clips at each end of permanent foldline, remove pattern, separate fabric layers, fold each with wrong sides together along fold line, using clip marks as guides, and press.

Make children's summer pyjamas out of fabric remnants. Cut each pattern piece in a different color for a wild look that kids love.

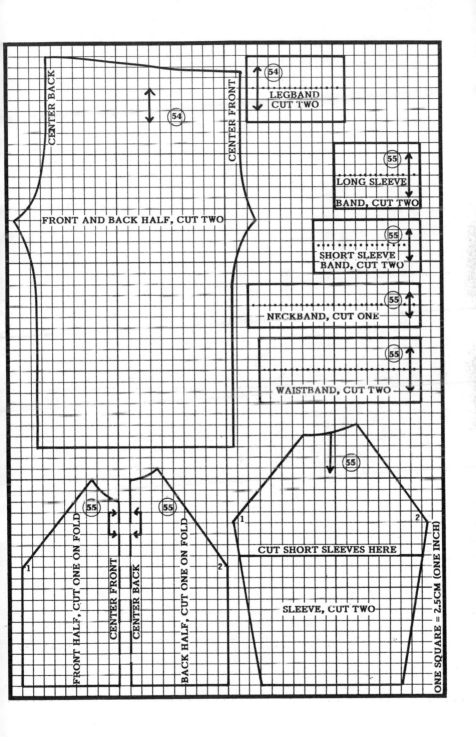

CENTER BACK

54

CENTER FRONT

FRONT AND BACK HALF, CUT TWO

54
LEGBAND
CUT TWO

55
LONG SLEEVE
BAND, CUT TWO

55
SHORT SLEEVE
BAND, CUT TWO

55
NECKBAND, CUT ONE

55
WAISTBAND, CUT TWO

55

FRONT HALF, CUT ONE ON FOLD

CENTER FRONT

CENTER BACK

BACK HALF, CUT ONE ON FOLD

55

1

2

55

1

2

CUT SHORT SLEEVES HERE

SLEEVE, CUT TWO

ONE SQUARE = 2.5CM (ONE INCH)

56. V-NECK DRESS (top, nightgown)
Size: 8

Short or long raglan sleeves, V-neck with band, elasticized waist, patch pocket.
Stretch fabrics only: Cotton knits, synthetic knits, stretch terry, velour. Also fleece. **Fabric required:** 140x115cm (1½ydx45"). **Notions:** Elastic for waist.

Sewing: Sew an appliqué or child's monogram onto pocket. Topstitch pocket in place. Stitch sleeves to armhole edges of front and back. Stitch sides and underarms. On inside, zigzag stretched elastic around waist. Overlock short sleeve ends, press them under 5cm (2") and stitch in place. Turn up a 2.5cm (1") cuff on sleeves and topstitch folded edge in place. (Stitch sleeve bands to long sleeve ends.) Sew neckband into a circle, clip corner until stitching line, press in half lengthwise wrong sides together and all raw edges even. Stitch the band around neck edge, stretching slightly to divide fabric fullness evenly. Overlock lower edge of dress, press it under and topstitch in place. (Make belt from braided fabric or rope.)

57. DRESS
(or nightgown, blouse and skirt)
Size: 8

Loose-fitting dress, short raglan sleeves, elasticized neck opening, elasticized sleeve ends and waist. Depending on fabric, trim sleeve ends and neck with rib knit bands instead of elasticized edge. (Lengthen the pattern for nightie. Or make blouse, and skirt with elasticized waist, lace trim.)

Suggested fabrics: Lightweight cotton types, seersucker, calico, broadcloth, Indian cotton, flannelette, pinwale corduroy, eyelet, cotton knits, velour, fleece. **Fabric required:** 120x115cm (1 1/4 ydx45"). **Notions:** Elastic (or rib knit), optional lace.

Sewing: Stitch sleeves to armhole edges of front and back. Stitch sides and underarms. On inside, zigzag stretched elastic to sleeve ends and neck, turn elasticized edges under and edgestitch in place. On inside, zigzag stretched elastic around waist. Overlock lower edge, press it under and topstitch in place. (Or, sew rib knit bands around sleeve ends and neck instead of elastic, gathering the fabric edge as necessary. Or trim edges with lace as for pattern #32.)

Make a no-cost embroidery hoop from a large plastic container with tight-fitting lid. Cut off and discard both the center of lid and the entire container below rim. Snap the remaining rims together like a hoop.

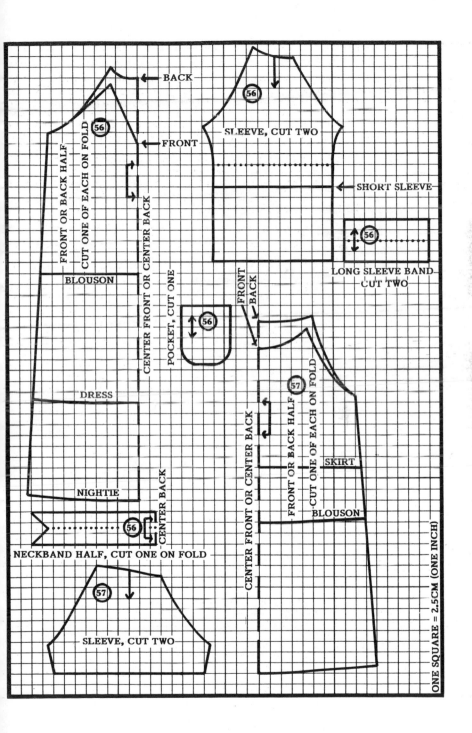

BACK

FRONT

56

FRONT OR BACK HALF

CUT ONE OF EACH ON FOLD

CENTER FRONT OR CENTER BACK

POCKET, CUT ONE

BLOUSON

DRESS

NIGHTIE

CENTER BACK

56

NECKBAND HALF, CUT ONE ON FOLD

56

SLEEVE, CUT TWO

SHORT SLEEVE

56

LONG SLEEVE BAND
CUT TWO

56

FRONT

BACK

57

CENTER FRONT OR CENTER BACK

FRONT OR BACK HALF

CUT ONE OF EACH ON FOLD

SKIRT

BLOUSON

57

SLEEVE, CUT TWO

ONE SQUARE = 2.5CM (ONE INCH)

107

58. COAT (or jacket, bathrobe)
Size: 8

Loose-fitting unlined design in three lengths, buttons or front zipper, hood (or rib knit neckband), patch pockets. Optional belt.

Suggested fabrics: Mediumweight cotton types, corduroy, denim, quilted fabrics, nylon (can be lined, if necessary, with flannelette or terry), wool duffle, windproof and water repellent fabrics. (Terry, stretch terry, velour for bathrobe.) **Fabric required:** 2mx115cm (2ydx45"). **Notions:** Interfacing, buttons or snap fastener tape (or separating zipper), interfacing, rib knit for neckband (for design without hood). (Jacket: Also cord for hood; rib knit for sleeve ends, waistband and pocket tops.)

Sewing: Iron fusible interfacing to wrong sides of facing allowances of front edges and hood. Prepare pockets and topstitch them in place. Stitch shoulder seams. Stitch sleeves to armholes. Stitch sides and underarms. Overlock sleeve ends and lower edge, press them under and stitch in place. Stitch hood center seam. Stitch hood to neck opening. Overlock front edges of hood and coat, press them under 5cm (2") and stitch in place. Make buttonholes and sew on buttons (or snap fastener tape, or separating zipper) on front. (If you wish, sew belt and belt carriers. Or, instead of belt carriers, sew belt casing from a separate piece of fabric to right side of garment.) Sew on rib knit neckband if you don't make hood; see pattern #42. (Jacket: Press on metal rings or make buttonholes in both lower ends of hood facing allowances, and insert cord through rings before stitching the hood front edge in place. Trim pocket tops with rib knit bands and topstitch pockets in place. Stitch rib knit bands to sleeve ends and waist. Sew zipper on front.)

Before you sew the garment, use a scrap fabric to check stitch length and the successful combination of needle and thread size.

If you need to apply fusible interfacing, cut the fabric piece first; then, using iron's tip, fuse a larger piece of interfacing to center of fabric's wrong side. Trim interfacing around fabric edges, press.

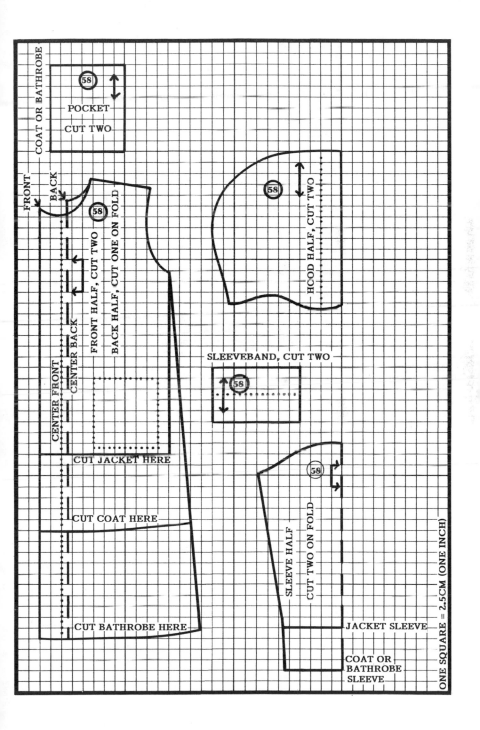

COAT OR BATHROBE

POCKET
CUT TWO

(58)

FRONT
BACK

CENTER FRONT
CENTER BACK
FRONT HALF, CUT TWO
BACK HALF, CUT ONE ON FOLD

(58)

CUT JACKET HERE

CUT COAT HERE

CUT BATHROBE HERE

(58)
HCOD HALF, CUT TWO

SLEEVEBAND, CUT TWO

(58)

(58)
SLEEVE HALF
CUT TWO ON FOLD

JACKET SLEEVE

COAT OR
BATHROBE
SLEEVE

ONE SQUARE = 2.5CM (ONE INCH)

109

59. NIGHTGOWN
Size: 8

Lace trim around butterfly sleeve ends, lower edge and wide neck opening. Mid-knee or ankle-length.
Suggested fabrics: Lightweight cotton types, seersucker, batiste, flannelette, cotton knits, fleece. (Flame-retardant fabrics are required by law on children's sleepwear. **Fabric required:** 210x115cm (2 1/3 yd x 45"). **Notions:** Lace.

<u>Sewing:</u> Stitch shoulder seams. Bind neck opening and sleeve ends with lace, folding the lace in half like bias tape. Stitch sides. Bind lower edge with lace.

60. T-SHIRTDRESS
(or top, nightgown)
Size: 8

Shoulders extend into cap sleeves with sleeve bands, elasticized waist.
Stretch fabrics only: Cotton knits, stretch terry, velour.
Fabric required: 1mx140cm (1ydx55"). **Notions:** Elastic.

<u>Sewing:</u> Stitch shoulder seams. Stitch neck facings into a circle, overlock outer edge, stitch facing around neck, press it to inside and topstitch in place. Stitch sides and underarms. Stitch each sleeveband into a circle, press in half right side out. Turn the garment inside out and stitch the bands around sleeve ends. On inside, zigzag stretched elastic around waist. Overlock lower edge, press it under and topstitch in place.

Instead of basting, use masking tape to keep zipper in place; stitch along tape's side, not through it.

Before applying zipper, stabilize stretch fabric edge with seam binding or fusible interfacing.

Turn store-bought garments inside out to see how and in what order the seams are sewn. These fast, professional shortcuts are equally handy for home sewing too.

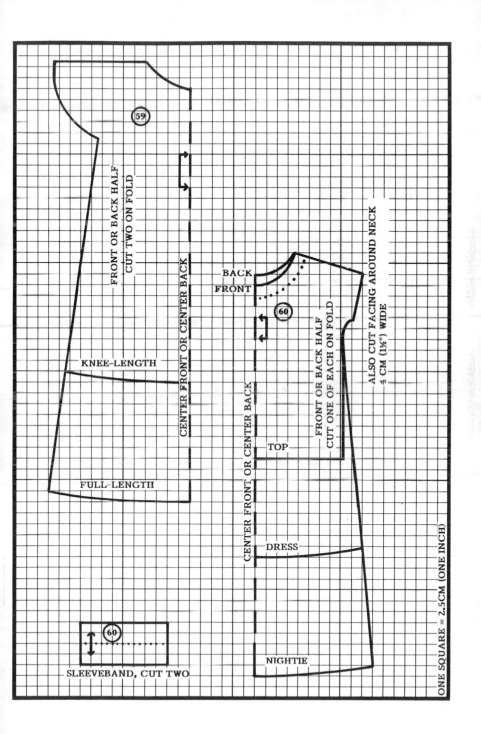

FRONT OR BACK HALF
CUT TWO ON FOLD

(59)

CENTER FRONT OR CENTER BACK

KNEE-LENGTH

FULL-LENGTH

BACK

FRONT

(60)

FRONT OR BACK HALF
CUT ONE OF EACH ON FOLD

ALSO CUT FACING AROUND NECK
4 CM (1½") WIDE

CENTER FRONT OR CENTER BACK

TOP

DRESS

NIGHTIE

(60)

SLEEVEBAND, CUT TWO

ONE SQUARE = 2.5CM (ONE INCH)

111

61. PANTS OR BERMUDA SHORTS
Size: 10

Loose-fitting pants or shorts with straight legs, elasticized waist casing and in-seam pockets.
Suggested fabrics: Cotton types. **Fabric required:** Pants – 210x115cm [2 1/3 yd x 45"]; shorts: 100x115cm [40x45"]. **Notions:** Wide elastic.

Sewing: Sew pockets to front and back side edges. Stitch side seams and curved pocket edges. Press seam allowances and pockets toward front. Baste pocket upper edges to the garment front. Stitch inner leg seams. Stitch center front and center back seams. Overlock waist edge and leg ends. Press waist edge under along the upper edges of pockets, stitch close to fold and along overlocked edge, forming a casing and insert elastic. Stitch vertically through all thicknesses at each seam [stitch-in-ditch] to prevent elastic from rolling. Hem leg ends.

62. TOP
Size: 10

Straight V-neck top with front yoke and short sleeves. [Consider using contrasting color, or fabric such as mesh, for yoke and sleeves.]
Stretch fabrics only: Cotton knits, stretch terry, velour. Also fleece. **Fabric required:** 70x115cm [3/4ydx45"].

Sewing: Stitch shoulder seams. Press neckband in half lengthwise right side out, and stitch it around neck, stretching the band slightly for neat fit; overlap ends at front and pin or baste in place. Stitch front section to yoke, catching neckband ends in the seam at the same time. Stitch sleeves to armholes. Stitch sides and underarms. Overlock sleeve ends and lower edge, press them under and topstitch in place. [Or make sleevebands and neckband from rib knit.]

Even oil gets old. If you bought your sewing machine oil years ago, it's time to buy a new bottle.

When both sides of fabric look alike or almost, stick a piece of masking tape to wrong side of all pieces while cutting. Pull the tape off immediately after sewing. [Be sure not to iron on the tape.]

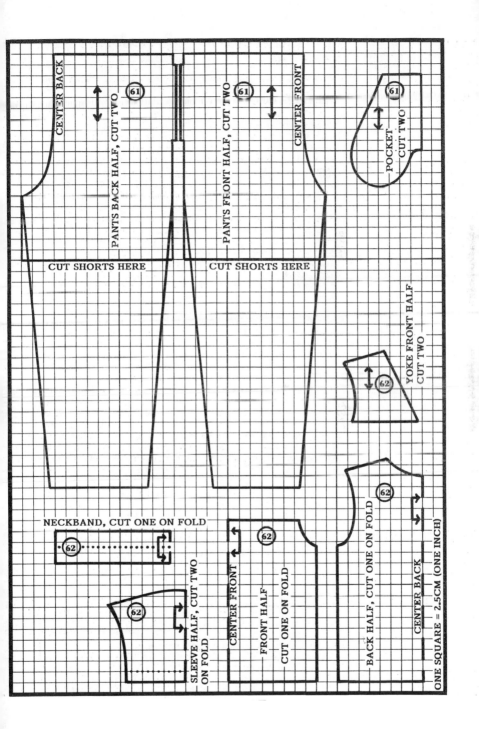

63. ANORAK
Size: 10

Hooded anorak with large flap pocket on front. Rib knit bands around sleeve ends and hood front. Hood and waist with cord drawstring. Front slit with zipper closure.

Suggested fabrics: Nylon, mediumweight cotton types, quilted fabrics, corduroy, denim, windproof and water repellent fabrics. (Or make this pattern from fleece, velour, stretch terry or synthetic knits, and make matching pull-on pants with pattern #61. Line the hood, if desired.)

Fabric required: 2mx115cm (2ydx45"). **Notions:** Elastic or rib knit for sleeve ends, rib knit for hood front edge (hoodband can also be made of self fabric), 250cm (2 2/3 yards) cord (cut in two for hood and hem casings), 15cm (6") long zipper, two buttons or snap fasteners or Velcro for pocket flap closure.

Sewing: Overlock outer edges of front facing. Right sides together, pin or baste facing to front. Mark front slit from neck edge 9cm (3½") down, stitch along both sides and across bottom end. Cut slit open between the stitching lines, press facing to inside and baste it in place. Overlock upper edge of pocket, press and stitch it under, sew on buttons or Velcro for closure. Press pocket sides and lower edge under and topstitch pocket in place 5cm (2") below front slit. Fold pocket flap in half lengthwise right sides together, stitch ends closed, turn right side out and press. Make buttonholes or sew on Velcro (to match pocket), stitch flap in place 2.5cm (1") above pocket. Stitch shoulder seams. Stitch center back seam of hood. Press facing allowances of hood center front under. Stitch the hood to neck opening. Stitch zipper in place (to front slit and hood front edges). Stitch hood band ends under narrowly, fold the band in half lengthwise wrong sides together and stitch it around face opening, forming a casing. Stitch sleeves to armholes. Stitch sides and underarms. Stitch rib knit bands to sleeve ends. Overlock lower edge. Make two buttonholes next to each other in the hem allowance at center front (or press metal rings through). Press lower edge under and stitch. Insert cords through hem and hood casings. Catch the cords in place with a few stitches through center back of casing so they won't slip out. (If you use quilted fabrics, bind front slit edges with doublefold bias tape instead of facing. Also bind pocket and flap edges with bias tape without turning the edges under.)

Use a sheet of typing or tissue paper under any soft or sheer fabric, lace, or mesh, if you have trouble stitching it.

114

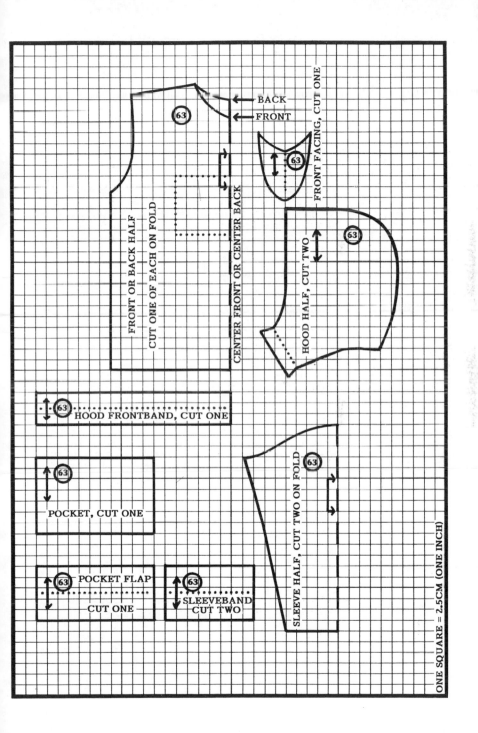

BACK
FRONT

FRONT FACING, CUT ONE

63

63

FRONT OR BACK HALF

CUT ONE OF EACH ON FOLD

CENTER FRONT OR CENTER BACK

HOOD HALF, CUT TWO

63

63 HOOD FRONTBAND, CUT ONE

63

POCKET, CUT ONE

SLEEVE HALF, CUT TWO ON FOLD

63

63 POCKET FLAP

CUT ONE

63 SLEEVEBAND
CUT TWO

ONE SQUARE = 2.5CM (ONE INCH)

115

64. ROMPER (or jumpsuit)
Size: 10

Pull-on romper with elasticized waist and upper edge, rounded side slits, narrow shoulder straps. (Jumpsuit: Sew romper top together with pants cut from pattern #61; shorten pants pattern at waist about 2.5cm/1".)
Stretch fabrics only: Cotton knits, stretch terry, velour. **Fabric required:** 60x140cm (2/3ydx55"). **Notions:** 150cm (60") long piece of contrasting doublefold bias tape (or bifold stretch tape made of self fabric; see page 35) for shorts sides and leg ends. Elastic for waist and upper edge.

Sewing: Sew shorts as for pattern #39, except waist. Stitch center back seam of top. On inside, zigzag stretched elastic to upper edge, turn the elasticized edge under and edgestitch in place. Stitch shorts and top together around waist. On inside, zigzag stretched elastic to waist seam allowance. Sew shoulder straps ready and stitch them in place under upper edge of front and back.

65. CAMISOLE (or dress, nightgown)
Size: 10

Tie-on shoulder straps and rib knit waistband. (Dress: Add single-layered snug waistband from rib knit, and gather miniskirt to its lower edge. Lengthen pattern for nightie with long side slits, omit rib knit waistband.)
Stretch fabrics only: Cotton knits, stretch terry, velour, rib knit. **Fabric required:** 60x115cm (2/3ydx45"), including enough fabric to make trifold stretch tape for neck edge, armholes and ties. **Notions:** Rib knit for waist 15x70cm (6x28").

Sewing: Stitch side seams. Stitch waistband into a circle, press in half right side out and sew it around waist. Cut stretch tapes of self fabric, two 5x23cm (2x9") for neck, two 5x75cm (2x29½") for underarms & tie ends. Press the tapes trifold (see page 35), bind upper edges of front and back with prepared tape. Middle of tape at side seam and ends extending into ties, bind underarms with stretch tape, edgestitching from end to end.

66. PULL-ON SKIRT
Size: 10

Elasticized waist casing, ruffle around lower edge, lace trim.
Suggested fabrics: Indian cotton, lightweight cotton types, eyelet, seersucker, cotton knits, fleece. **Fabric required:** 70x115cm (3/4ydx45"). **Notions:** Wide elastic for waist, lace or eyelet trim.

Sewing: Stitch center back seam. Stitch ruffle into a circle, trim lower edge with lace, gather upper edge and stitch it to skirt's lower edge. Stitch waist edge down into a casing and insert elastic.

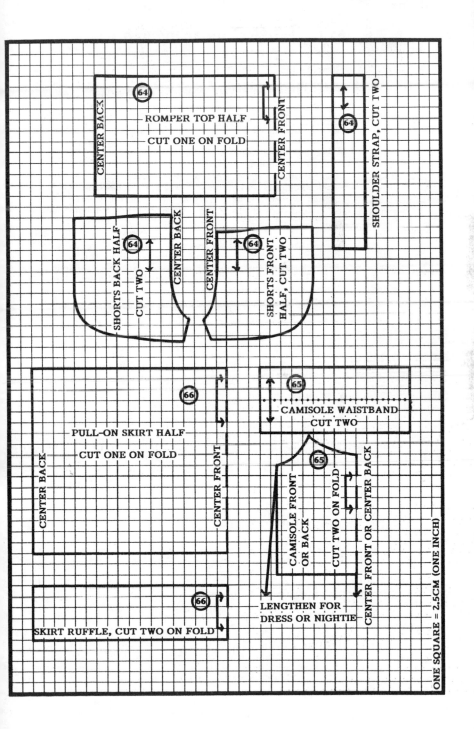

CENTER BACK
64
ROMPER TOP HALF
CUT ONE ON FOLD
CENTER FRONT

64
SHOULDER STRAP, CUT TWO

SHORTS BACK HALF
64
CUT TWO
CENTER BACK

CENTER FRONT
64
SHORTS FRONT HALF, CUT TWO

66
PULL-ON SKIRT HALF
CUT ONE ON FOLD
CENTER BACK
CENTER FRONT

65
CAMISOLE WAISTBAND
CUT TWO

65
CAMISOLE FRONT OR BACK
CUT TWO ON FOLD
CENTER FRONT OR CENTER BACK
LENGTHEN FOR DRESS OR NIGHTIE

66
SKIRT RUFFLE, CUT TWO ON FOLD

ONE SQUARE = 2.5CM (ONE INCH)

117

67. JUMPSUIT (or sleeveless top, dress, nightgown, knickers)
Size: 10

Sleeveless, knee-length jumpsuit with elasticized waist and leg ends, self stretch binding around neck and armholes. (Cut top, dress, nightie or knickers, as shown in the pattern. Knickers: Elastic at waist, rib knit bands around knees, or leg ends gathered to kneebands tied at side, see #4. Top: Sew rib knit band around lower edge. Dress: Zigzag stretched elastic below waist, blouson style. Nightie: Add rounded hemline slits.)

Stretch fabrics only: Cotton knits, stretch terry, velour. **Fabric required:** 120x115cm (1 1/4 ydx45"). **Notions:** Elastic for waist and knees; contrasting, doublefold bias tape (or trifold stretch tape, see page 35) for armholes and neck.

Sewing: Stitch left shoulder seam. Bind neck edge with stretch or bias tape. Stitch right shoulder seam. Bind armholes with stretch or bias tape. Stitch side seams. Stitch center front and center back seams of pants. Stitch inner leg seams. Stitch pants and top together around waist. On inside, zigzag stretched elastic to waist seam allowance. Zigzag stretched elastic to leg ends, turn elasticized edges under and edgestitch them in place.

For an easy-to-move seam guide, slip a rubber band around your sewing machine's freearm.

Cut folded fabric with right sides together whenever possible so center seams are ready to stitch together.

The more you sew, the better you get and the easier it will be.

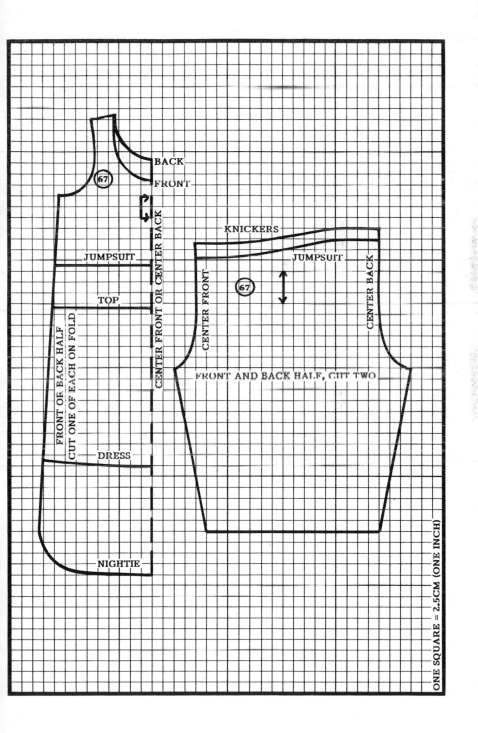

BACK

FRONT

67

JUMPSUIT

TOP

DRESS

NIGHTIE

FRONT OR BACK HALF
CUT ONE OF EACH ON FOLD

CENTER FRONT OR CENTER BACK

KNICKERS

JUMPSUIT

67

CENTER FRONT

CENTER BACK

FRONT AND BACK HALF, CUT TWO

ONE SQUARE = 2.5CM (ONE INCH)

119

68. SUMMER DRESS
Size: 10

Flared skirt gathered to top. Shaped, slightly dropped
waistline.
Stretch fabrics only: Cotton knits. **Fabric required:**
160x115cm [1 3/4 yd x 45"].

Sewing: Stitch shoulder seams. Stitch bodice side seams.
Overlock raw neck edge and armhole edges, press them
under and topstitch in place. [Topstitching with double-
needle looks good.] Stitch skirt side seams. Gather skirt
upper edge and stitch it to the bodice. Overlock lower
edge, press it under and topstitch in place.

69. TOP
Size: 10

Roll-up kimono sleeves, kangaroo pockets, front opening
and ties.
Stretch fabrics only: Cotton knits, stretch terry, velour.
Also fleece. **Fabric required:** 120x115cm [1 1/3 yd x 45"].

Sewing: Overlock bias edge of each pocket, stitch them
under. Press upper edges under and topstitch pockets
in place [pin or baste sides and lower edges in place].
Stitch center front seam from lower edge upward, at
the same time catching pocket edges in the seam; leave
10cm [4"] open at neck edge. Press seam allowances of
front opening and center front seam under and topstitch
in place. Stitch shoulder seams. Cut a 1 metre [40"] long
strip of fabric, press it into trifold [see page 35]. Stitch
the prepared tape around neck with ends extending on
each side for ties. Stitch sides and underarms. Overlock
sleeve ends and lower edge, press them under and topstitch
in place.

Cut basic patterns from interfacing to use them
repeatedly. Some stores even sell interfacing printed
with one inch grid [or with dots spaced an inch apart].

Don't buy fabrics **printed off-grain** since they are
impossible to correct. Fabrics that are **pressed off-
grain,** can be straightened by dampening and stretching
on the bias; press if necessary.

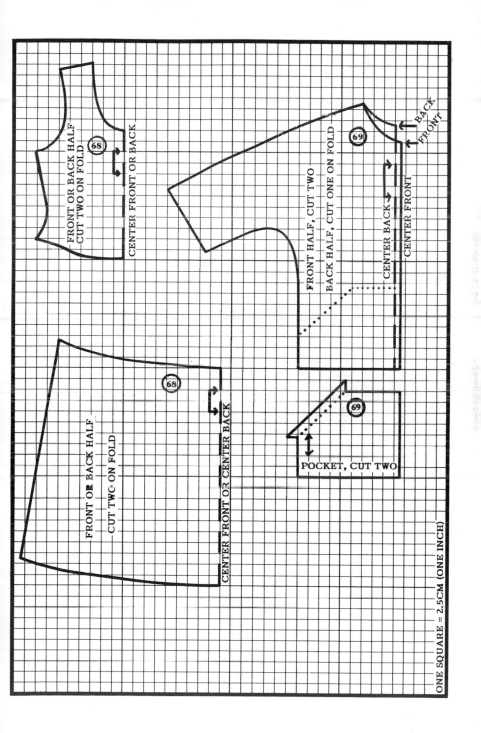

FRONT OR BACK HALF
CUT TWO ON FOLD

68

CENTER FRONT OR BACK

FRONT HALF, CUT TWO
BACK HALF, CUT ONE ON FOLD

69

BACK
FRONT

CENTER BACK

CENTER FRONT

FRONT OR BACK HALF

CUT TWO ON FOLD

68

CENTER FRONT OR CENTER BACK

POCKET, CUT TWO

69

ONE SQUARE = 2.5CM (ONE INCH)

121

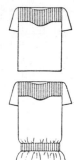

70. TOP (or dress)
Size: 10

Double-layered rib knit yoke at front and back. Short sleeves. (Add single-layered rib knit waistband and ruffled skirt for a dress.)
Suggested fabrics: Cotton types, cotton knits. **Fabric required:** 1mx115cm (1ydx45"). **Notions:** Rib knit.

Sewing: Right sides together, stitch shoulder seams of yoke 7½cm (3") in from each side toward neck (as shown in the pattern), lock the stitch securely at neck edge. Turn right side out, each yoke in half, so you have the neck opening in the middle. Stitch front and back sections to double-layered yoke. Stitch sleeves to armholes. Stitch sides and underarms. Hem sleeve ends and lower edge narrowly.

71. DOLMAN TOP (or dress)
Size: 10

V-neck top with shoulders extending into 3/4-sleeves, self bands or rib knit around waist and sleeve ends. (Cut striped fabric on the bias. Lengthen pattern for minidress and stitch stretched elastic below waistline.)
Stretch fabrics only: Cotton knits, stretch terry, velour. **Fabric required:** 1mx115cm (1ydx45"). **Notions:** Self fabric or rib knit for waistband and sleevebands 15x110cm (6x44").

Sewing: Stitch shoulder seams. Stitch neck facings together into a circle, overlock outer edge, stitch facing around neck, press it to inside and topstitch in place. Stitch sides and underarms. Sew bands around sleeve ends and waist.

Reduce noise and prevent sliding by placing a rubber-backed carpet piece under your sewing machine. Get a suitable piece free from your local carpet dealer's discontinued samples. Another piece under foot-pedal will prevent it from sliding on uncarpeted floor.

Clean your overlock machine with a narrow bottle brush. Then vacuum through a narrow funnel that has extra long tip (tape on a piece of straw for extension if necessary), to get maximum suction.

Doublefold bias tape makes quick drawstring ties: edgestitch the tape closed from right side through all thicknesses.

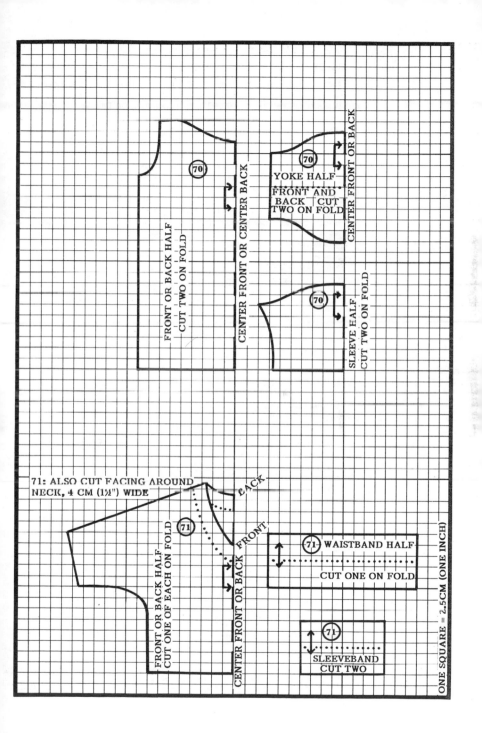

FRONT OR BACK HALF
CUT TWO ON FOLD

CENTER FRONT OR CENTER BACK

CENTER FRONT OR BACK

YOKE HALF
FRONT AND
BACK CUT
TWO ON FOLD

SLEEVE HALF
CUT TWO ON FOLD

71: ALSO CUT FACING AROUND
NECK, 4 CM (1½") WIDE

BACK

FRONT

FRONT OR BACK HALF
CUT ONE OF EACH ON FOLD

CENTER FRONT OR BACK

71 WAISTBAND HALF
CUT ONE ON FOLD

SLEEVEBAND
CUT TWO

ONE SQUARE = 2.5CM (ONE INCH)

123

72. PONCHO
Size: 10

Hooded poncho with separating front zipper, buttons under arms.

Suggested fabrics: Warm, soft fabrics, such as wool duffle, thick corduroy, wool blends, tweed, thick knits. Lightweight, absorbent fabrics for summer poncho to wear over swimsuit, such as terry, stretch terry, velour, fleece. Nylon, windproof and water repellent fabrics, or vinyl with flannelette lining, for rain poncho. **Fabric required:** 160x115cm (1 3/4 ydx45"). **Notions:** 65cm (25") long separating zipper, doublefold bias tape or foldover braid, four large buttons.

Sewing: Cut center front open from neck to hem. Stitch hood center back seam. Stitch hood to poncho around neck edge. Bind hood front edges, poncho front and lower edges with bias tape or foldover braid. Stitch zipper in place. Sew buttons on under arms as shown in the pattern, back and front buttons sewn together through the fabric. Or, instead of buttons, topstitch under arms as for cape #47. (If desired, decorate poncho with appliqués, fabric paints, or decorative ribbons.)

73. NIGHTGOWN (or blouse, dress)
Size: 10

Loose-fitting nightgown with short or long sleeves, elasticized self ruffles around sleeve ends, ruffles inserted in sleeve seams.

Suggested fabrics: Lightweight cotton types, flannelette, seersucker, batiste, eyelet, Indian cotton, cotton knits, velour, fleece. (Flame-retardant fabrics are required by law on children's sleepwear.) **Fabric required:** 230x115cm (2½ydx45"). **Notions:** Elastic, optional lace.

Sewing: Stitch shoulder seams. Stitch neck facings together into a circle, overlock outer edge, stitch facing around neck, press it to inside and topstitch in place. Trim sleeve ends with lace or hem them narrowly. On inside, zigzag stretched elastic to sleeve ends, 5cm (2") from lower edge, forming self ruffles. If not cut along selvage, narrowly hem the straight edges of shoulder ruffles (or bind them with folded lace), gather curved edges and stitch them between sleeves and garment, stitching sleeves to armholes at the same time. Stitch sides and underarms. Overlock lower edge, press it under and stitch in place.

> Clean your old spiral mascara brush with cleaning lotion or oil, then thoroughly wash with soap and water. The brush is great for removing lint and fuzz under throat plate and around bobbin.

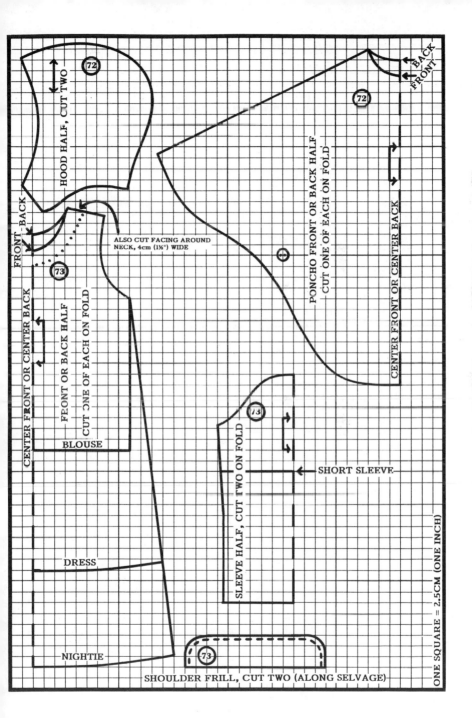

HOOD HALF, CUT TWO

72

FRONT — BACK

72

BACK
FRONT

PONCHO FRONT OR BACK HALF
CUT ONE OF EACH ON FOLD

CENTER FRONT OR CENTER BACK

CENTER FRONT OR CENTER BACK

ALSO CUT FACING AROUND
NECK, 4cm (1½") WIDE

73

FRONT OR BACK HALF
CUT ONE OF EACH ON FOLD

BLOUSE

73

SLEEVE HALF, CUT TWO ON FOLD

SHORT SLEEVE

DRESS

NIGHTIE

73

SHOULDER FRILL, CUT TWO (ALONG SELVAGE)

ONE SQUARE = 2.5CM (ONE INCH)

125

74. JUDO-STYLE PAJAMA PANTS
Size: 10

Elasticized waist casing, no side seams.
Suggested fabrics: Cotton types, flannelette, also cotton knits, stretch terry, velour, fleece. (Flame-retardant fabrics are required by law on children's sleepwear.) **Fabric required:** 120x115cm (1 1/3 yd x 45"). **Notions:** Wide elastic for waist.

Sewing: Stitch center front and center back seams. Stitch inner leg seams, sewing crotch piece in place at the same time. Overlock leg ends, press them under and stitch in place. Overlock waist edge, press it under and stitch it closed forming a casing, insert elastic.

75. PAJAMA JACKET (or bathrobe)
Size: 10

Short or long sleeves, front buttons, patch pockets. (Wrap-around bathrobe has tie-on belt.)
Suggested fabrics: Cotton types, flannelette, cotton knits, stretch terry, velour, fleece. (Flame-retardant fabrics are required by law on children's sleepwear.) Also terry for bathrobe. **Fabric required:** 120x115cm (1 1/4 yd x 45"). **Notions:** Four buttons.

Sewing: Prepare pockets and stitch them in place. Stitch shoulder seams. Stitch sleeves to armholes. Stitch sides and underarms. Press sleeve ends under 1cm (3/8") and again 2.5cm (1"), and stitch them in place. Stitch front bands together at center back, fold the band in half lengthwise right side out, and stitch in place to front edges and around neck, stretching slightly for neat fit, press. Press the lower edge under (like sleeve ends) and stitch in place. Make buttonholes and sew on buttons. (Bathrobe: Belt will stay in place better if, instead of belt carriers, you make a belt casing from a separate piece of fabric and stitch it to the right side of fabric across back waist from side seam to side seam.)

Press as you sew.

Have your children make large envelopes for your patterns out of their school papers and drawings. A great way to save both!

To make new from old, check if the fabric is reversible. The wrong side might look like new even if right side is worn, faded and linty.

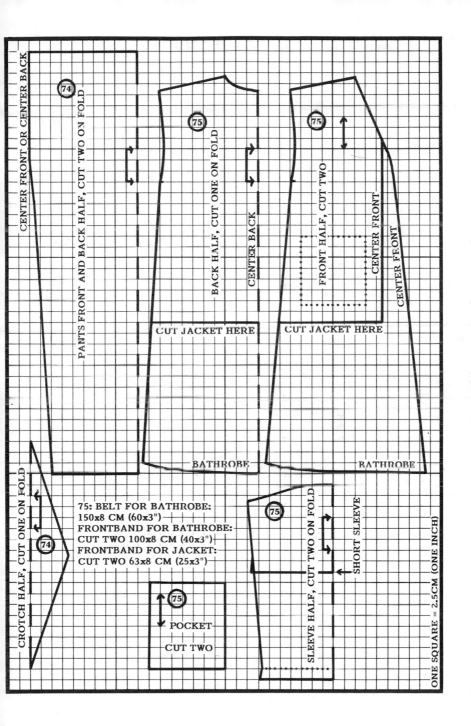

CENTER FRONT OR CENTER BACK

74

PANTS FRONT AND BACK HALF, CUT TWO ON FOLD

75

BACK HALF, CUT ONE ON FOLD

CENTER BACK

CUT JACKET HERE

75

FRONT HALF, CUT TWO

CENTER FRONT

CENTER FRONT

CUT JACKET HERE

BATHROBE

BATHROBE

CROTCH HALF, CUT ONE ON FOLD

74

75: BELT FOR BATHROBE:
150x8 CM (60x3")
FRONTBAND FOR BATHROBE:
CUT TWO 100x8 CM (40x3")
FRONTBAND FOR JACKET:
CUT TWO 63x8 CM (25x3")

75

SHORT SLEEVE

SLEEVE HALF, CUT TWO ON FOLD

ONE SQUARE = 2,5CM (ONE INCH)

75

POCKET

CUT TWO

127

BE A PART OF MY BOOKS

Realizing that some of the best ideas might come from my innovative readers, I am inviting your comments and suggestions.

If you have great sewing tips or other suitable ideas that you would like to share, I would love to hear from you. Should I use your idea in one of my books, I will send you a complimentary, autographed copy of that book. Write to: Leila Albala, ALPEL PUBLISHING, P.O.Box 203, Chambly, Quebec J3L 4B3, Canada.

NOTES _____

_____

_____

_____

_____

_____

_____

_____

_____

_____

_____

_____

_____

MEASUREMENT CHART

For a handy reference, record here the measurements of your child/children. Use a pencil for easy changes.

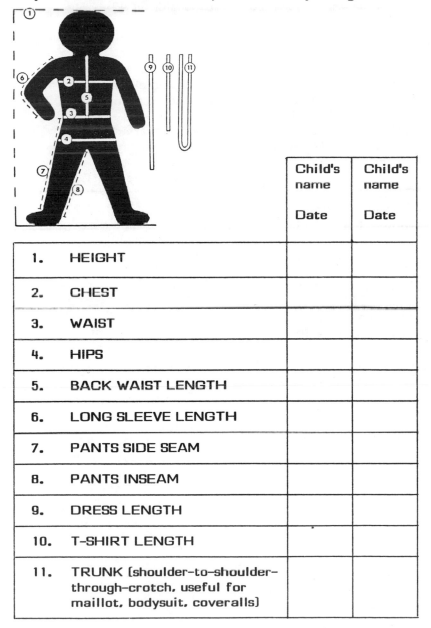

		Child's name	Child's name
		Date	Date
1.	HEIGHT		
2.	CHEST		
3.	WAIST		
4.	HIPS		
5.	BACK WAIST LENGTH		
6.	LONG SLEEVE LENGTH		
7.	PANTS SIDE SEAM		
8.	PANTS INSEAM		
9.	DRESS LENGTH		
10.	T-SHIRT LENGTH		
11.	TRUNK (shoulder-to-shoulder-through-crotch, useful for maillot, bodysuit, coveralls)		

INDEX

GLIMPSES OF THE AUTHOR

From her childhood days in rural Finland, making tiny garments for dolls, through teen years sewing her own designs for friends, and on to adult life designing and sewing for pleasure and business, Leila Albala has combined her love of creative sewing with practical wearability. Upon graduation from Finnish commercial college, Leila worked in several European countries, gaining experience in a variety of jobs. When she and her husband, Elie, came to Canada in 1973, they founded their own mail order business, named ALPEL. Their self publishing business started in 1982. While sewing constantly for her children, Albert and Rina, Leila developed her own patterns and an easy way to design and print them in miniature. Her first book, "Easy Sewing for Infants", became an instant success after it was featured in Family Circle, Vogue Patterns, and dozens of other magazines. Thereafter, positive feedback from her readers inspired Leila to continue the series with "Easy Sewing for Children", "Easy Sewing for Adults", and "Easy Halloween Costumes for Children". Her next title will be "Easy Sewing for Teens".

Author photo by Elie Albala

132